WOUNDED by BETRAYAL
A GUIDE TO PERSONAL EMPOWERMENT

*Looking for Love in All The Wrong Places
Could Lead to an Addictively Destructive Life*

WOUNDED by BETRAYAL
A GUIDE TO PERSONAL EMPOWERMENT

La'Donna R. Edmond

Wounded by Betrayal: A Guide to Personal Empowerment
La'Donna R. Edmond.-1st ed.
Copyright © 2011 by ESounds Publishing

This title is also available as an EVE/ESounds audio product.
Visit www.LADONNArEDMOND.com for more information.

ESounds Publishing
P.O. Box 750605
Houston, TX 77275

Library of Congress Catalog Number: 2011940982
ISBN-10: 0983791007
ISBN-13: 9780983791003

Copyright © 2011 by La'Donna R. Edmond. All right reserved.
No part of this publication may be reproduced, distributed, or transmitted in any form or by any means, including photocopying, recording, or other electronic or mechanical methods, without the prior written permission of the publisher, except in the case of brief quotations embodied in critical reviews and certain other noncommercial uses permitted by copyright law. For permission requests, write to the publisher, addressed "Attention: Permissions Coordinator," at the address below.
EVE / ESounds Publishing
P.O. Box 750605
Houston, TX 77275

Ordering Information:
Quantity sales. Special discounts are available on quantity purchases by corporations, associations, and others. For details, contact the publisher at the address above.
Orders by U.S. trade bookstores and wholesalers.
Please visit www.ladonnaredmond.com or Email: info@ladonnaredmond.com.

Printed in the United States of America

Contents

Dedication... IX
Author's Letter to Love XI

Wounded By Betrayal

Prologue.. XIII
   Mind Made Up!.... *xv*

Chapter 1

I Need Out—"Motivation of the Author" 1
   Damaged Goods.... *1*
   Background Experience of the Author *4*
   My Childhood as the Baby Girl *4*
   First Heartbreak *13*
   My First Love.. *15*
   Second Ex... *19*
   My Intentions and Parental Background *23*
   Addiction of the Author................................. *25*
   Truth be Told *30*
   Back in the Day–My Attempts to Move on *32*
   Awakening to Recovery *33*
   I Need Out *35*
   Benefits of Conquering your Addiction *37*
   Preparing for your Road Trip! *38*

Chapter 2

Ready For Change—"Setting the Ground Rules" ... 41
   Understanding Why You are Making the Change........ *41*
   Mystery Behind the Rules *51*
   Abiding by the Rules *53*
   Misery & Aloneness.. *57*
   Accepting that You are Going to Hurt *59*

    Understanding Your Body 62
    Crying is the Best Gift of Healing 64
    Prepare for Distractions 65
    Get Fed Up! 69
    Quest for Revenge 71
    Understanding how You Became Addicted 74
    Final Preparation for the Road Ahead 77

CHAPTER 3

DETOXIFYING YOUR FOCUS 81
    Focus 81
    New Territory 83
    Emotional Rollercoaster Ride... 85
    The New Guy, Ex #3 86
    Polygraph Test 96
    Getting it all out of Your System 101
    Where to Go From Here 105
    Be Mindful of Distractions 109
    Environment 109
    Communication 111
    Music 113
    Pandora's Box 114
    Don't Skip a Beat 115
    Reflection 119

CHAPTER 4

LEARNING THE NEW YOU & FINDING YOUR TRUE VALUE ... 123
    The Healing Continues 123
    All in the Fragrance and Soundtrack 124
    Admiring Yourself 129
    Learning Yourself 130
    Sexual Appetite 134
    Finding your True Value 137
    Good Efforts are Never Made in Vain 139
    Make You Happy First 143

Valuing Your Worth *146*
Placing Value on Your Hard Work *149*
Recap *150*

Chapter 5

CAUTION EMPTY PURSUITS & EMPTY PROMISES 153
   What If? *153*
   Empty Pursuits *156*
   Empty Promises *157*

Chapter 6

PRODUCT OF YOUR ENVIRONMENT 167
   Hidden Obstacles in Stifled Growth *167*
   The Generational Cycle of Life *170*
   Root of the Matter *175*
   Covering all Bases *183*
   Positive Figures *185*
   The Conclusion *187*

Chapter 7

STAGES OF LIFE TRULY LETTING GO 191
   No Regrets! *191*
   Developing Stages in Life *194*
   Carry Your Cross *196*
   Each stage is a building lesson to your growth: *197*

Chapter 8

DATING AGAIN 199
   Welcome to Dating 101! *199*
   Now, for the Rules! *202*
   Blind Date *205*
   Just be Yourself *211*
   Have Fun *212*
   Judge *215*
   Telltale Signs *217*

   Sex *218*
   Not Ready to Date yet? *220*
   Conclusion *220*

Chapter 9
Life Goes On 223
   Routine Maintenance for Guaranteed Satisfaction *223*
   Flesh vs. Spirit *226*
   Freedom in Forgiveness *227*
   End to my Exes *228*
   Maintaining Happiness *230*

Acknowledgements 233
About the Author 237

Dedication

As human beings, we constantly are seeking some form of satisfaction. Satisfaction can be derived from a need or desire, but the end result is pursuant to satisfaction. When the constant need to feel satisfied turns into an unhealthy addiction, the desires give birth to desperation and dissatisfaction. Sometimes, we are so consumed with worldly pleasures and building treasures that we forget that the true treasure resides within our own hearts.

I dedicate this book to those lost and desperately craving satisfaction in their lives. I especially want to reach out to those feeling trapped in confusion or disappointments caused by betrayal, toxic relationships, or unhealthy addictions. I pray that this book may help you find the freedom to take advantage of limitless opportunities and give you the discipline to maintain a healthy life.

Faith, Deliverance, Peace, and Love

Author's Letter to Love

Dear Love,

I have found beauty in your purest form and fulfillment in your energy. It deeply grieves my heart to see people dilute you for convenience and greed or mistake you for infatuation. This dilution often is turned into to an imitated substitute of your kind, but doesn't stand the test of time when paralleled to your endurance. It disappoints me even more to see that people allow the diluted, substitute version of you lead their lives and dictate their actions. Most end up unhappy or completely opposed to finding you again. They lose sight of your healing and stray from your forgiveness. If only we would yield to your purity, we could find your infinite level of peace. You have the power to unveil the truth and lead us successfully on in life even through the most undesirable setbacks. Thank you, Love, for unveiling your beauty to me.

Love Always,

LaDonna R. Edmond

WOUNDED BY BETRAYAL

Prologue

The purpose of this book is to help those who are addicted to satisfying their fleshly desires find deliverance and hope. This venture will be explained in a way that will allow those who are addicted to toxic relationships understand how to overcome their addiction, through control, while providing the knowledge to overcome almost any addiction. It starts from the inward willpower that we must realize causes each and every one of us to relent to whatever pleasures our fleshly desires. Are you addicted to love, lust, sex, porn, homosexual behavior, procrastination, eating, alcohol, drugs, shopping, clutter, coffee even? I laugh as I write such ridiculous addictions like coffee and clutter, but you all must understand that such addictions are real and have an effect on the way we live. Addictions are simply that which give us temporary pleasure or satisfaction. I hope you noticed the word "*temporary*," which suggests addicts are never completely satisfied.

Addictions can work as an antagonist to the livelihood of our life stories and justify the actions from which we seek pleasure; this is why addicts are never truly content. In reality we all are looking for pleasure; we just need to make sure it's healthy. I believe everyone is addicted to something; however, controlling that addiction will maintain balance for a successful life. Control is the act of managing or exercising authority over the limitations of something; it is a form of power. Too much of anything can be detrimental, and anything worth having is worth working hard for and persevering through to the very end. Each one of us, without being in self-denial, knows what is too much. We are all individuals for a reason and have different thresholds of tolerance for everything. Our goal is to realize them and move forward without hurting others for selfish gain in the process. I will use the terms "OUR" and "WE" a lot in this book because I want you all to realize that no one is perfect, including me. Just because you have fallen into a lifestyle of social and emotional un-acceptance, to either society or yourself, doesn't mean you are less than the next person. I too struggle with my own vices, but have learned how to control and balance them by setting boundaries in order to live a healthy life. Again, I use the terms "OUR" and "WE" as a reminder that fighting addictions is an ongoing battle with the self, to remain successful in everything we do, and you are not alone. Remember, the goal is success! We want success within ourselves, relationships, careers, and most importantly our LIVES! Building a solid and knowledgeable foundation allows you to navigate your way through life with the wisdom to understand how to live your life with balance and a healthy focus. Imagine that, a world full of well-balanced, disciplined, and emotionally healthy people! All I can say is WOW to that! Either way, whatever decisions you decide to make for yourself, please realize *why* you are making them, and don't allow your emotions to make these decisions for you. Relying on emotions is a sure road to an unhealthy life. Never act from emotions.

MIND MADE UP!

Understand that as you read through this book, the only way it will assist you successfully, is if you have already made up your mind to make a change. Ultimately, you can not make a change if:

- You do not know what needs to be changed.
- You are still in denial and unwilling to accept your addiction as a problem.

If you are reading this right now, I think I can assume that you already have determined within yourself to cross that line of scrimmage. This book is not designed for those who are interested in excuses about why they cannot move forward, or why they cannot move on, or how their situation is so much worse than the next person. I'll save that topic for another book! Instead, by choosing to pick up this book, you are choosing to journey successfully through a healing process. We are at the point in our lives where change is necessary to live, because it's the only way to make you a better person. Even though it's difficult to change, once you are there, you'll see clearer and will be able to guide others through your experience, just as I am doing right now!

CHAPTER 1

I Need Out
"Motivation of the Author"

DAMAGED GOODS

For many years, I was thought to be damaged goods. I didn't know how I had fallen into emotional depression and completely lost hold of myself and my focus. In a matter of two years, I felt my life dwindle down to mere meaninglessness. I used to be beautiful, spontaneous, energetic, and most of all, an emotionally healthy woman. I was a singer, I was creative, and I also had the drive for success to add to it. I was full of dreams, which I sought to conquer. I was the woman that men dreamed of being with, and women wanted to be like. I used to be happy. I used to have control over my life, my finances, my goals, my actions, my flesh, and even my temptations. Suddenly, it seemed that after life took its toll on my undisciplined behavior, I found myself lost in a world of addictive entrapment. My mind, the very entity that ruled my physical existence, was captivated by demise. What happened? How can a person of such high caliber allow herself to become diminished to such a level, so low, so fast?

It was the agonizing pain of withdrawal, from being stripped away from my addiction, my partner, and my balance that planted me in a state of confusion within myself. When I shared myself with my partner, I lost a piece of my individuality to him. Just imagine someone ripping your body in half and you not being able to do anything about it but endure the pain. How torturous is that? I endured this torture, but in a spiritual and emotional manner. After becoming stripped of my individuality, I was linked, and then became addicted, to partners who were incompatible to my morals. The pain from depression and disappointment caused a door to open to things that took advantage of my vulnerability, causing even more misery, because misery loves company. This misery was an epidemic to my emotions, and I turned into damaged goods.

My first mistake was entering into serious relationships before ever learning the importance of understanding my own emotions or myself. I, unknowingly, drove myself into this turmoil, with the assistance of my infamous accomplices, my partners, whom I trusted to have my best interest at heart. Instead, they didn't care enough to protect my emotional well-being. Every experience I attached myself to affected me deeper and deeper, which resulted in my becoming miserable. It seemed impossible to break myself from this state of misery. All I knew was that I didn't like how I felt; however, unbelievably, I continued doing exactly what made me feel dissatisfied and confused. If I tried abandoning my addiction it hurt, and if I stayed it hurt. Either way, I was so deep into confusion that whatever decision I made, it simply hurt like hell.

It's now very clear to me that the intimacy of love is not a recreational sport; rather, it's a connection to our divine frequency. In a relationship, when you share yourself with your partner, you expose your most fragile internal makeup, the core of your heart. By exposing your divine core, you become vulnerable to possible disappointments and even heartbreak, which could lead to various addictions. In most cases, you are unaware of just how far you have fallen or succumbed to the addiction of whatever pulls you away from what was your own personal reality, until you hit rock bottom. When I hit rock bottom, my depression was a product of an unstable foundation, and I naively was following the unstable flesh. My own personal reality became a figment of my imagination, which led me to a frail existence. This emotional decline changed the way I handled my business. I stopped caring about everything around me. I didn't care about my appearance, health, or weight. There is certainly a thin line between love and hate because in that moment, the love I used to have for myself reflected the exact opposite. I confidently can say now that we all should recognize that line instead of just ignoring it until the inevitable happens.

WOUNDED *by* BETRAYAL

BACKGROUND EXPERIENCE OF THE AUTHOR

I've had three long-term relationships, all of which drew me to the many obstacles, and later the solutions that I'll share with you. My experiences went from good to bad, and when I didn't think it could get any worse, it did. As I approached each new experience, I simply brought my baggage from one relationship to the other, without first cleansing myself from the previous relationship. I sabotaged my relationships before they even had a chance to blossom into healthy experiences. Without realizing it, I allowed each new experience to change me. Unfortunately, they somehow changed me for the worse because I approached each new relationship from the emotional level I was on at the time. Blindly looking for the relationships to validate stability and save me from my disappointments of betrayal, I ended up surrendering my power in exchange for havoc. Though my experiences trapped me in unwanted turmoil, eventually I saw the light at the end of the tunnel and found my escape. Each of my relationships taught me very valuable lessons, which now have opened the gateway to emotional and mental freedom, not only for me, but others as well. In an effort to conceal the identities of my exes, I will not address them by their names.

MY CHILDHOOD AS THE BABY GIRL

My dad called me "Babygirl" growing up because I was the youngest girl out of six kids. My parents had four boys and two girls, and I was the fifth born. My little brother Chris and I always stood out because we were the only fair skinned, kids in the house. The rest of the family, including Mom and Dad, had dark brown complexions. Adonis, the fourth born, was extremely dark, the darkest in the house. My family joked that he stole all the chocolate pigment, because after he was born, the last two came out with no "color." As the baby girl, I always got a lot of attention from my family because they always felt they had to look out for me. I had dark brown eyes, thick eyebrows, and thick golden brown hair that grew right past my shoulders. I always combed my hair in a ponytail because it was the only style I could do by myself and still look decent enough to hang with my older siblings and their friends. I didn't have many friends of my own because I preferred the love and attention my family and their friends gave me instead.

Whenever I was caught idle, you'd see me holding my ear, rubbing it with my fingers while sucking my tongue as if I had a pacifier in my mouth. This brought a level of comfort that somehow relaxed me as a child. I'd even put myself to sleep doing it sometimes; it became my habit. My dad always said I looked so cute when I played with my ear because I had this soft innocent look in my eyes, which made him just want to hold and protect me forever. That same look created a soft spot in my Mom's heart for me. I always was able to convince her to take me to work with her instead of day care, more times than I think she realized. All I would have to do was hold my ear and give her the look. I loved going to work with my mom; it was the only time I could have one-on-one time with her. She taught special needs students, and everyone loved her because she had a gift of healing and could motivate people into doing the impossible. I'd just sit and watch her work her magic with her students. She was a great teacher, and I could tell her students respected and admired her.

My brothers adored me and looked after me when my dad was away. I was fortunate to have four brothers, but even more fortunate that three of them were older, because they were able to guard me growing up. Don was ten years older, Gabriel was four years older and Adonis was one year older. Chris, on the other hand, was almost two years younger than me. Nonetheless, I was protected from every angle. Don never really had much to say and no one my age ever crossed him because he was so much older than me. Instead, Don was the brother who provided for me in the absence of my parents. If I got sick in the middle of the day, he picked me up from school and made sure I was cared for properly. When my parents did not have enough money to put me through certain activities in school, Don was the brother that secretly paid my way, so that his baby sister would not miss out on important activities.

My brother Gabriel ruled with an iron fist and protected me with the most intensity. I remember, in third grade, he stayed up all night preparing me for my solo line in a school play. He didn't go to sleep until he knew I had my line memorized. The next day, when it was time for me to recite my line, I proudly walked up to the microphone, took a deep breath, began to speak, but suddenly forgot my line in front of everyone. I panicked and ran off the stage. Although Gabriel was disappointed that I had forgotten my lines and walked off the stage in the middle of the program, he still comforted me in the end and assured me that I would do better next time. Once I reached my adolescent years, I hated how strict he was with me. He had a heavy influence on my mother, and often times I had to seek his approval to do anything, even to wear certain clothing. He fought to preserve my innocence and took his role as "big brother" extremely seriously. He taught me how to recognize bad guys and would constantly drill me on the appropriate way a female should act around males. To this day, I still feel indebted to him.

Adonis always stood out, not only because of his fierce, dark complexion, but because he was the most talented in the family. He was extremely artistic and was able to master anything he put his mind to. He had a natural, raw talent. He taught himself how to draw and play the piano in grade school. He was a fan of Wolverine from X-Men, and drew the cartoon character, which had everyone in awe. His understanding of line symmetry was impeccable, especially for his age and having had no training. He was an exceptional singer, the family comedian, and the fighter. Adonis never backed down from a fight; in fact, his first fight was when he was in third grade. Some sixth grader tried to bully him, and that day he learned how good of a fighter he was. From then on, he was the brother who fought for me if any guy ever got out of hand. Fortunately for me, he was also the brother with whom I went to school. I loved going to school with Adonis because I would piggyback off of his popularity. If it were not for him, people in school probably would not have known who I was. Because of his comical personality, unique artistic abilities for singing, and knack for fighting, people seemed to flock to him, and he was popular anywhere he went. For this reason, some of my peers referred to me as, "Adonis' Lil Sister."

Chris was always the quiet and compassionate brother. He always studied his environment and learned from the mistakes of those he followed, which in this case happened to be all 5 of his older siblings. Fortunately for him, he actually did not have to do anything, when it came to my protection, because Don, Gabriel and Adonis had established reputations that created respect for the Edmond brothers. My sister, LaQuanda, always seemed to pull out the best in me. I called her "My Sista" throughout our childhood because I had difficulties pronouncing her name as a little kid. My sister was awesome; she taught me how to put on makeup, match my clothes, and even comb my hair. When I was a kid, she would let me play in her makeup even though it was about four shades darker than my skin color and I was forbidden to wear it. She would always laugh at me when I put on the finishing touch of her pink, flavored lipstick. I loved the smell and taste of her lipstick; it tasted like bubble gum candy. Intoxicated by the fragrance, I would always rub way too much on my lips and it would smear past my lip line and all over my face. I wanted my makeup to look just like my sister's because she was so pretty and glamorous. I dressed up in all of her cool clothes, even though they were too big for me, in anticipation of owning them one day when she grew out of them. She knew I looked up to her, and that alone made her proud, protective and careful with me. My sister had a mind of her own and

I Need Out—"Motivation of the Author"

always remained two steps ahead of me. She predicted my moves and provided me with direction from her experiences as a young woman. She looked out for me and gave me advice from a young perspective, and because she was five years older than me, I did not deem her advice to be old-fashioned. She made sacrifices by giving up certain things in her life, to make sure I did not lack the things I needed growing up in my life.

I remember the year I started band class. My parents could not afford to buy me a brand new instrument, so my dad gave me $100 dollars to buy a used flute. I walked to the EZ Pawn shop around the corner and found an old, used flute for $99 dollars. Thankfully, the salesman did not make me pay taxes! Although I had no idea what to look out for and my options were limited, it was the only flute I could find with the money I was given. At the time, I thought it was a great deal, even though the casing was badly beaten up and the inside was falling apart. The flute was tarnished from old age but the salesman said it worked, and that's all I really cared about. I actually was proud of myself for finding what I thought was a good deal and I couldn't wait to learn how to play it, well, until I took it to school. I soon learned that I got what I paid for because the flute did not play any flat notes. The first six weeks I failed band class because of the flute's inability to play accurate notes. A flat note in music is like a vowel in the alphabet, you need it to properly piece things together to make sense. I would go home everyday, sad and embarrassed at the sound that came out of that flute. It was unnatural and sounded pitiful; even my band teacher hated my flute, but I never gave up.

WOUNDED *by* BETRAYAL

One day my band teacher blasted me out in front of the whole class when she found yet another deficiency with my flute. Not only could this flute not play flat notes but it also was bent out of shape. I remember this particular day in band class because it was chair test day. Once a week, the band teacher selected a piece of music for each student to play individually in order to determine which chair we would sit in based on how well we played. First chair was reserved for the best player while the last chair was for the kids who did not practice, or were not very good. Out of about seven flute players at the time, I believe I was in chair four or five, which was pretty good considering my flute's deficiency. My band teacher stood on the podium right in front of me and tilted her head sideways, as if she was assessing the condition of my flute. Suddenly, she asked, "Why is your flute crooked?" in a loud, demeaning manner. I sadly remarked, "I don't know, I bought it this way," and she just stared at me after my response, as if she was lost for words. I was extremely embarrassed; she had just announced to the whole class that my flute was raggedy. It did not help that the classroom was completely silent at the time, which just made the sting from the insult that much more memorable. I used to play this flute with my head tilted to the right most of the time so that no one would notice how badly it was bent out of shape. That day my band teacher stamped her place in my memory for the rest of my life; I was humiliated in front of my peers. That was the last day I carried that flute to band class.

The same day, my family gathered together for what looked like a spontaneous party. I just figured we all were celebrating family unity again. This particular time, the attention was turned towards me, and I had no clue why. I remember my sister telling me to play this cadence called "Go, Team, Go." I was not sure why she wanted me to play my flute because everyone in the house hated the sound of it but my sister remained pretty adamant about me playing this tune for the family. So, my mom went to the back room to grab my flute and came back to the living room and handed me my old, beaten up case. When I opened the case to grab my old flute, I was extremely surprised to see a brand new, sparkling silver, Armstrong imprinted, flute, which was blinding me with beauty and ready to be played. I blinked in amazement and absolutely was stunned and at a loss for words. My impression was frozen, as my eyes widened and my mouth dropped to the ground as if I were screaming but without a sound escaping my vocal cords. My heart began to beat ecstatically, and I was caught between reality and fantasy as I tried to figure out how this was possible. I was not sure what was going on until my sister spoke up and said, "Play your flute, Qual." My family called me Qual (pronounced as "Kell"), short for ReQual, which is my middle name. I looked up at my sister and glanced around the whole living room to bask in this moment as all my family watched my expression of joy. Jumping out of mental shock, I grabbed my new flute and assembled it excitedly. It was so smooth and flawless, and assembling it was even more inviting because all of the pieces fit together perfectly. This was my first time playing a brand new flute, and the sound was ever so pure. I played the first few notes of the requested cadence and when it was time to yell "Go, Team, Go!" my whole family yelled, "GO, QUAL, GO!" instead, with their hands in the air in support of my talent! I cried tears of joy that evening.

My sister worked at Ryan's Family Steak House restaurant, and had been saving up her tip money to buy me that brand new $500 Armstrong flute. Through her unselfish gratitude and desire for me to be the best, I finally experienced being the first chair flute player. Truth be told, I realized, after playing my new "flawless" flute, how much effort I was putting into the old flute in order to produce a somewhat decent sound. I loved being the baby girl because a day didn't pass that I didn't feel loved by my family.

My parents embedded family values and love in every phase of our development. They constantly drilled us about the importance of being grateful for each other. We were a singing family, so during the holidays my Mom would take the six of us to local nursing homes to sing carols. We loved singing, and they loved inviting us. We were also a praying family and very active in the church. If the car didn't start on Sunday morning, we all walked to church together. We were not allowed to miss Mass on Sunday mornings, so we all woke up early to avoid unexpected setbacks in order to make it to church on time and keep Mom happy. After church, Mom cooked and we all sat at the table, as a family, and ate together. We were taught that family had to remain loyal to each other, no matter what, and so that made us all grow up very close. We always put each other first because we were taught family came first. These

I Need Out—"Motivation of the Author"

were generational values our parents expected us to continue. I soon learned that in order to truly protect the love I had for my family, abandoning, neglecting, or betraying it was forbidden. Through loving my family, I grew an entitlement to love. I figured that if I put the person I loved first, then they too would do the same for me if they loved me. I loved the way love felt and I never wanted to detach from it. Loyalty was my biggest requirement when it came to love. I never thought about being betrayed by those who claimed to love me because the only love I had experienced thus far was from family, and I knew they'd always be loyal to me, the baby girl. In my eyes, at that time, I lived in a perfect, protected world.

First Heartbreak

Things changed when my parents divorced and our family broke up. I was seven years old. I never had a problem sharing my dad with family and friends as long as I knew we were still his number one, which he always made known. I even was able to deal with him dating other women. It wasn't until a year later, when I heard another kid other than my blood siblings call my dad "Daddy," that I felt my first sting of betrayal. There I stood, an eight-year-old kid, holding my ear, hair pulled back in a ponytail, confused, with tears in my eyes, a large lump in my throat, and a cold, numb sensation running through my heart, feeling as if I had been replaced. The truth was that I still hadn't fully accepted the fact that my dad no longer lived with us and we were no longer a family. In

WOUNDED *by* BETRAYAL

my mind the title of "Daddy" was superior and honoring; only those worthy should have the privilege of referring to him in such a manner. It was painful because it seemed as though each new lady friend of his had daughters who seemed to think it was okay to call my dad "Daddy." They only diminished the title in my eyes. I had a big problem with that because I did not want them to be my sisters. I had my own sister, one who I knew would be there for me till the end of time. We were loyal to each other through blood. The effects of my parents' divorce had begun burdening my feelings. I began feeling as though something very important was taken away from me, and I became territorial by instinct. I was forced to share something of mine that I felt was not supposed to be shared. I couldn't understand why I had to share my dad, in what I felt was a sacred capacity, with absolute strangers. It felt insulting to me, and for my dad to allow it added more pain to injury. I felt cheated, like all the love and attention my father once had given me now was shifted towards his new lady friends and their children. I didn't know why I felt this way; I just did. I was experiencing my first heartbreak, and I didn't even know it. My only hope was growing up and one day finding a love of my own that would never leave or replace me. As a growing adolescent, and in the stages of dating, I carried that same entitlement with me into my relationships, hoping to be my partner's only one and never having to share him with anyone else. I hated the thought of betrayal through cheating, so I looked for loyalty and love in my partner. Strangely enough, I found it in my first love!

I Need Out—"Motivation of the Author"

MY FIRST LOVE

I started dating my first love at the age of 16. I was a junior in high school and also worked part-time at the local Best Buy. One afternoon he came into Best Buy as a customer and I remembered him because he was in my fourth grade summer camp, about seven years back. Back then, he was a chubby sixth grader and he had an enormous crush on me. When I saw him that afternoon, he was all grown up and far from chubby. Our attraction to each other was instant. We exchanged numbers and started dating soon after.

I used to ride the city bus to work from school and often times would get off of work after 10 p.m. Since the city bus stopped running at 9 p.m., I looked for alternative ways to get home. Sometimes I was lucky enough to catch a ride with co-workers. I faithfully was saving my money in the hopes of purchasing my own transportation one day but was not quite there yet. My safety was my first love's main concern, and it burdened him to know that some days I was stranded at work. He went so far as to borrow his parents' vehicle to pick me up from work and take me home even though he knew they had grown agitated from his frequent requests to borrow their car. We lived on completely opposite sides of the town, so he'd have to borrow the vehicle for at least an hour and maybe an hour and a half, if we wanted to spend a little time with each other. Over time, and through his constant burden of securing transportation, he decided to purchase a vehicle we both utilized, to drive me to and from school and work every day.

My First Love showed me how a good woman should be treated by the way he loved me. He never allowed a day to go by without expressing how special I was to him. I was his number one, and I knew it. He even knew how to cook full course meals. He'd cook lunch for me so that I was able to eat a healthy, home-cooked meal during my lunch breaks, and he made sure it was hot and fresh when he brought it to me at work. He always surprised me with a dozen roses, candy, cookies, cards, and love letters, just because. He would surprise me so often that I had to ask him to stop or slow down because I grew to feel entitled to those things, and it became a right instead of a privilege. Special occasions became everyday events because he constantly surprised me, which in effect, diminished my gratitude for the treatment. He truly took good care of me and lavished me with unconditional love through my senior year of high school.

He had graduated from high school a couple years prior, and we were one year and nine months apart in age. Everyone thought we were moving way too fast in our relationship because on Saturday, November 27, 1999, my first love proposed to me. I said "yes," hoping to get married sometime after college because I was only 17 and still in high school. He, on the other hand, wanted to get married sooner than that, but our families were not too fond of that idea. On Monday, July 23, 2001, my first love tattooed our names, locked with a heart and rose, on his right upper arm as an initiation, because he was certain we'd be together forever. Family and friends all knew he was crazy in love with me, but everyone felt we were too young to have such an intense relationship. I was still Babygirl to my family, and his family felt as though he was too young to settle down.

The reserved feelings our families had, unfortunately, added doubt to our relationship, and we began looking for flaws in each other. We surmised because we had different religions, we were yoked unequally. Eventually, our union separated because, in our eyes, we were too young to realize the uniqueness and value of what we had. Therefore, we did not protect it. We both felt that we had our lives to find, and we eventually split after I left home for college. He soon covered his tattoo with what I believe was a large blue flower. When he showed it to me, I was incredibly hurt, because I knew that he had truly moved on and there was no chance of us getting back together. All I could do was cry from disappointment, and in that moment of hurt, the only comfort I found was an old picture I had taken of the tattoo before he covered it.

Several months later, I found out he was engaged. Stunned by this news, I called him. I had no idea what I would say if he picked up. All I knew was that I needed to say something one last time because I still believed he was my soul mate. I stood in an empty dark room, closed my eyes, and dialed his number. He picked up within the first ring, saying, "Hey, Baby," in a deep warm tone. By the sound of his voice, I knew he was content and in his comfort zone. I was speechless because that's what he used to call me, and I knew he was not expecting me to be on the other end of the phone. He continued calling out, "Baby," "Baby," and "hello?" He sounded as if he was in an empty room too, because there was almost an echo in his voice. Then there grew silence, and at that moment I knew that he knew it was me on the other end of the phone. Still shocked by his expressions, I finally conjured up enough nerve to say something. I said "hi," in a frail, lifeless tone as my heart beat ecstatically. Confirming his hunch with my voice, he responded to my greeting with "hi," in return, and then asked, "How did you get my number?" I explained myself, and he did not take any time to inform me that he was engaged. Strangely enough, I still was stunned and stuck on the beginning part of our conversation. I could not get my thoughts together for the life of me. Therefore, I pretended as if I did not know he was engaged. I was confused and caught between nerves, pride, and how I was supposed to be reacting towards the man I still loved, in concert with the fact that I had no direction in my spontaneous impulse to calling him. I did not know if I was supposed to act happy and congratulate him, or reveal my true feelings and attempt to convince him not to go through with it. I immediately went into panic mode and dropped all masks of strategies. I spoke to him with my heart, and expressed to him that I took marriage very seriously, and that if this were something he really wanted to do, he permanently would build a wall that would separate me from him, a forbidden wall, which I could never attempt to cross to reach him because this move would permanently seal him to her through God's power. I humbly, but desperately, asked him if he was sure about the decision he was about to make. Stalling for a few moments, he finally answered in a soft and cautious tone, "yes."

At that moment, I felt my life was taking an unfamiliar but permanent twist, for which I was unprepared. Disappointed, I immediately fell to my knees in grief, and curled myself on the floor, closing my eyes while the tears ran down my face. I mourned in the unsettling reality in which his response had placed me. I knew that he knew I was hurting on the other end because there was complete silence for several moments. I also knew that he still had feelings for me, so I tried to understand his reasoning for marrying so soon. I asked if she was pregnant, and he said no. At that point, I had to wish him well, let it go, and try to move on with my life. I hung up telling him, "This time, I can't fight for you." He was willingly surrendering himself to another woman and I had no choice but to accept it.

Second Ex

My second relationship had its good times, but most times were bad. We started dating before I was emotionally over my first love. My love addiction coupled with my desire to have companionship ultimately held me captive in that relationship. We met in college and he became my tutor. At first, he showed absolutely no interest in me. To break the ice, I actually had to ask him if he was gay because he'd never picked up on my slight advances. I'd show up for our one-on-one tutoring sessions smelling extra nice, and sat extra close to him, when clearly there was room for distance. It was very obvious that I liked him, but he never picked up the hint. It was strictly schoolwork with him, and that was it. He had a real nerdy appearance and wore tape on each side of his glasses to keep them together, and he wasn't even ashamed. For some crazy reason, I dug his style and loved the fact that he was private and did not care what people thought of him. I referred to him as an original nerd because of the taped glasses and the fact that he was incredibly smart. I figured that with a little cleaning up, he really could be some good eye candy! I thought he had great potential but just needed to come out of his shell, and that's what provoked my desire to nurture him. Because he was so quiet and mysterious, I wanted to know more about him without coming on too strong. Going against the teachings of my big brother Gabriel, I went out on a limb and made the first move by telling him how I felt. He had no idea that a girl like me ever would be interested in him. At first, I was flattered by his initial lack of interest because it made him challenging to me. I thought he was guarding his heart, and I wanted to win the key. After making the first move, by expressing my feelings, we started dating. Most days seemed to be a challenge with this guy, a challenge I hardly found appealing after two years of dating.

Two years into our relationship, I learned it was not his heart that he was guarding; instead, it was something else he was trying to conceal. I also learned that my happiness was not on his priority list. Instead, random social chat lines and Internet chat rooms were the focus of his attention. He claimed that he needed to network, and that it was the best way to meet new people in order to jump-start his career as a new college graduate. It struck me as

I Need Out—"Motivation of the Author"

being very odd that I was never introduced to these "professionals." I also found it strange that they always were random and only seemed to call at non-business hours, for non-business purposes. I knew he was up to something because his alibis never satisfied my suspicious intuition. I had had enough when the random friends began stealing our quality time and excuses took the place of our scheduled plans. At first, I had no clue as to what was going on because he seldom dealt with the same person twice. It took me becoming very attentive and watching his moves to find out what he was truly up to. The Internet became a place where he could be whomever he wanted to be because no one held him accountable on the Internet. My feelings told me this man was being dishonest but he'd plead and cry out that my feelings were wrong. He was so convincing that he made me feel out of place for questioning his loyalty. It was difficult to break up with the one I loved, when in my mind, I was not supposed to leave because I loved him. I had to be loyal to this person but at the same time I felt as though I was betraying my own intuition and feelings. Something inside of me begged me to leave him, but another part of me wanted to feed from this mysterious lust. Soon, it all unfolded, and the truth revealed itself to me. I must say that I definitely was not prepared for what I was about to find out.

I had decided to snoop around for answers, allowing my intuition to lead me to what I felt I needed to see. Allowing me full access, I looked through his video collection, cell phone, and email, and what did I find? I learned that he not only had met and slept with random women, but also entertained inappropriate, questionable, sexual conversations with men, too. I grew highly convinced that he was a down-low brother. Though he denied being gay, I found it strikingly odd to be put in situations where we were arguing about late-night phone calls and sexual communication with random gay men. I felt as though he was either lying or in denial to himself by thinking that he was not gay because he openly dated and copulated with women. Later, I noticed his strange collection and unhealthy supply of pornography. He collected strange films I never knew existed and I was quite rattled. I felt that all the signs were there, but he never confirmed my uncertainty. However, I was certain that I had fallen for a sexual maniac. I was scared for my health and my life, and I ultimately felt betrayed. This is where my cycle of depression magnified. How do you recover from such a heavy blow after finding this kind of information about the person whom you trust and love?

 I was caught in his web and knew I needed to get out to save my life but I couldn't. I had become addicted to his companionship and mixed up in the love/lust relationship we had. As long as he denied all dealings with men, I was able to pretend that I never saw the inappropriate conversations, just so I would not have to deal with the pain of separation. I thought that maybe if I did certain things for him, which were not too demoralizing to my morals, he would not need to outsource to the Internet and chat lines. I figured, now that it was all in the open, perhaps he would stop hurting me. I thought that maybe I should lighten up a little bit; perhaps,

I Need Out—"Motivation of the Author"

I was not adventurous enough for him. Eventually, I conditioned myself to believe that my standards were too high, and so I succumbed to his will of bondage, in the name of love. Still fighting with the truth and myself, I was at war in my own being. He had such a convincing tongue and I did not want to feel abandoned. I had become dependent on his companionship. At that point, I just wanted someone to care, to love and never betray or leave me. I was addicted to love and did not want to become a sellout by betraying it. I knew my love was real and I felt that I had to prove it by sticking it out to the very end. I thought I could change him by showing him true love, and so I continued to forgive him every single time he cheated. The hurt from that relationship is what started my deep thinking process, not to mention that I had no choice considering the fact that my love had turned into desperation. Desperation was now opening me up to a new world of confusion. My thoughts alone were enough to keep me busy for ages.

MY INTENTIONS AND PARENTAL BACKGROUND

Originally, this book was intended to reach out to all teenagers who felt as though they were trapped in a relationship from which their young, developing hearts could not seem to break away. It was not until I did some self-reflection of my own that my eyes were opened. I was not a young teenager withdrawing from the loss of my first love anymore. I was in my second serious relationship, growing into adulthood, and started understanding why women called all men dogs. I had firsthand experience as to how one person could spoil it for the rest. This cliché was quite fitting for many; however, because my first serious relationship experience was quite pleasant (talk about setting the bar for the rest), I knew without a shadow of doubt that there was in fact hope for a healthy life, a faithful relationship, and true love. My father once told me that I had inherited a heart of passion and because of it, when I love, I love deeply; it is a love that undoubtedly penetrates to the absolute core of my heart. I guess that contributed to why I had put up with so much in my relationships.

My mother remained a single woman after the divorce and overcame her own personal addiction to the temptation of the flesh. As a young follower, I was able to glean from her success, absorbing all of her wisdom and healthy morals. We were not a wealthy family by any stretch of the imagination, and therefore had to rely on faith, after the divorce, in order to maintain motivation for success. I had an intensely religious grandmother. She and my mom would pray together all night long. It was as if the whole family lived off of their prayers. My mother and grandmother, thankfully, introduced me to the spiritual world.

They made sure to feed me wisdom that ultimately became my foundation of faith, love, and truth. Fortunately, due to their prayers and this foundation of truth, I felt an immense sense of guilt every time I moved in the wrong direction and sunk deeper into depression. I was also uncomfortable in this unhealthy lifestyle of emotional bondage. Every time I felt that sense of guilt, an internal gleam of light from truth was released and I was able decipher what actually was taking place within my mind and soul in order to begin healing and uproot my decline. With this awareness, I immediately began to dig my way out but found that it was much harder than I thought. It was as if everything was against me and my biggest setback was myself, because even though I wanted out logically, every other entity of my existence wanted in emotionally. I felt hopeless with the solution to my unhealthy, addictive relationship problem. It was as if I had the key to success, but could not open and walk through the door to my victory because my addictive nature imprisoned my growth and was stronger than my will to actually make a move. Realization was half the battle. Once I realized that the addictive cravings connected my emotions to an unhealthy life, I recognized the antidote that would cure it. If it could not cure it, it would at least treat it so that I wouldn't sink deeper into other addictions, and deeper into depression. At that point, I just wanted to turn my depression around.

ADDICTION OF THE AUTHOR

Two years turned into three, and three years turned into four, and the abuse from his behavior was not getting any better. Four years into this emotionally-damaging relationship with my second ex, I just wished there was something like a book or movie that would help me through this breakup, which eventually became a rollercoaster addiction. We went through many spells of breaking up and then getting back together. During the breakup periods, we never completely left each other alone, and I tried dating other people in order have a Plan B in place. My failed attempts to secure another partner provoked me, by default, to go back to my second ex every single time. It was clear I could not break away with my own will, but that did not stop my conscience from reminding me of my failure and depressing my existence. I was not experienced in how to heal heartbreak, and I was never taught how to deal with a heartache. I focused so much on the relationship and my partner that unconsciously it consumed me. I not only wanted out, I also wanted to successfully heal from the pain and residue that had matured inside of me. This pain and residue eventually resulted in me developing the attitude of an indignant woman who once was filled with adventure, innocence, and hope, but now was angry, and consequentially wounded by betrayal again.

The deception I faced was that the breakup would be difficult, when in actuality, breaking up was the easy part. The difficult part was staying gone after the breakup and remaining true to my decisions and words. It took years to figure that part out. My mind tricked me into believing that I could *not* function without my partner because I had allowed my emotions and flesh to take over, control, and live for me. Because my emotions wrapped me in this unhealthy relationship, I felt as though I should stay and just be miserable with this man that possessed me. Like the song says, by the late Luther Vandross: "I'd rather have bad times with you, then good times with someone else," right? WRONG. As you can see, I was not whole or rational, and I felt as though I could not live without my partner during the break-up days. It was emotional torture. My emotions and I were withdrawing, like a fiend on crack, while contemplating my conscience: *"Maybe this time he'll change; it's been almost two weeks; he should've learned his lesson by now."* I even started selling myself short with, *"Well, I know he slept with her, but what the hell; I'm not fed up yet, I'll just take him back eventually anyway."*

I started feeling as though I was the one trippin'. What was I thinking? *This man loves me; he'd never betray me. Just trust him*; I'd tell myself. I did not have any proof, but I knew something was changing inside of me. I began experiencing abnormal sexual desires through this silent exposure. I always was taught that homosexuality was an immoral, shameful act. However, I was faced with the shame of simply desiring something that was forbidden and embarrassing. I fought with myself: Is it right? Is it wrong? I beat myself up over this growing, shameful desire while wondering, where is this coming from? It felt as if he had planted a seed within me and his lifestyle nourished it. All the while he was practicing this promiscuous lifestyle, he'd return home completely unaware that he was not alone. He'd bring home to me a piece of each one of his partners, which were just more distractions for the relationship to battle with, especially if "we" were trying to work things out.

I'm a firm believer that we all must be careful as to what we entertain and what doors we open and expose to our lives, because they just may lead to destructive lifestyles. Your lack of preparation could set you up for failure, because what you don't know *can and will* hurt you. I struggled to clean the additional residue from myself, not only what he'd contributed, but that of his several new partners. If it wasn't a new position, it was a new look (i.e., a wig) to make me different. I tried everything to keep him happy, otherwise it resulted in boredom. The different cravings of his growing appetite alone were overwhelming and difficult to satisfy. Through this exposure, I unconsciously adopted an appetite of my own, and he wondered why I was steadily declining to a life of emotional bondage. The dysfunction simply became acceptable to me. It was a battle, which was taking its toll on me, in every shape, form, and fashion. I was beginning to change the person I was, so much so that I did not even recognize myself anymore.

I changed all right, for the worse. I began to self-destruct because I alone could not rid myself of the relationship. I was torn between satisfying my fleshly desires and upholding my moral values; it was quite unsettling and I was far from content. I was ashamed to expose the severity of my addiction to anyone, especially my family, because I kept going back. If they knew how weak I had become, they would question my sanity, give me the "are you crazy" look, and make me feel even worse then I already felt. Subsequently, after time had passed, I began trying things that I said I never ever would try, while continuing my downward spiral into depression. Please understand, for those of you who feel as though your behavior resulting from an emotional disaster has caused you to accept things and a lifestyle you'd rather not expose or that is inconsistent to healthy living, I do understand, and this book is definitely for you.

I Need Out—"Motivation of the Author"

I hit rock bottom emotionally and felt I had nowhere else to turn. Either I revel in this lifestyle that I clearly knew was unhealthy for me, or do something different.

While under the influence of depression, I began to think about the value of my worth, my dreams, my goals, and my happiness. I also began to think and wonder whether other people went through the same experience I was going through. I felt horrible, to the point where I did not even enjoy the company of myself. I hated being alone. I even started to hate myself for allowing myself to get so emotionally unstable and uncomfortable, and felt it must be something I was not doing right, or perhaps I must not be good enough. As if to say that giving one's heart, such an invaluable gift, was not good enough. How could anyone conceive that thought?

I began to question my meaning for living and started hating anything that reminded me of one of the women with whom he had cheated on me. If a certain color, car, age bracket, or business company reminded me of the hurt or the woman, I hated it. I hated the thought of betrayal, too. After all, betrayal is what ultimately had put me in this empty position. Betrayal found pleasure in borrowing another woman's man. Betrayal broke up my happy childhood. Betrayal did not care about boundaries, discipline, or respect. I hated betrayal with a passion, and resented the world around me for tempting us with things that provoked betrayal. I was confused. I did not even want him anymore, but I kept going back because I wanted what I was striving to obtain, companionship. I did not particularly care for the pain his companionship rendered, but hey, it was companionship.

I started judging and categorizing women and the world around me. I had become a bitter woman at the age of 21, at a time where life should have been unwrapped and discovered through the eyes of an eager, emotionally healthy, and ambitious young woman. I also understood why there were so many bitter women in the world. Perhaps they too had been violated by betrayal. I began to isolate myself from the world, and even from my family. I felt ugly, possessed, and weak; it just hurt, to say the least. I cried all the time and could not find a way out of the madness. I started believing the different things my second ex would tell me, like that I was insecure, unsuccessful, psycho, crazy, unstable, inconsistent, but most of all, that he loved me throughout the emotional abuse.

Truth be Told

Don't get me wrong, my second ex remained a nice guy. He was a handy man and always held down a good job and came home every night. He listened to me express myself, most of the time, and took good financial care of me while I was going through college and did not have a job. From the outside looking in, it appeared as if we had a successful and promising future together. He already had graduated from college with top honors, and I was soon to follow him by completing my bachelor's degree in accounting. He wasn't the typical "bad man;" you know, the type who physically abuses his partner and doesn't take care of the home. Part of the problem was that he wasn't the typical bad man I'd hear about on talk shows

I Need Out—"Motivation of the Author"

or from other friends. I figured that it was all the more reason to stay, because I had something promising, right? Wrong again! That thought process was only a way to suck me in even deeper. The honest truth is that bad partners come in all shapes, sizes, colors, and cultures. It's really about compatibility, integrity, and the endurance of one's heart that determines a good or bad partner. I did not realize this at the time. I say now, where the hell was my value? It was still there, somewhere; I just had lost focus from it. Instead, it was his intelligence, humble personality, and nerdy appearance that made me feel secure and safe. Now that I think of it, I guess it made the others feel safe, too.

I was so emotionally disconnected that all the next guy had to do to impress me was show me a little attention, take me out on a date, and actually pay for it, if he wanted to sweep me off my feet. Do you see the level to which I had succumbed? I mean really, I was that impressed by a man who'd pay to take me to Bennigan's restaurant, a movie, and open a door for me on our first date, that I was willing to incautiously open my heart in the hopes of falling in love again. Forget about his conversation or getting to know him. I was stuck on the fact that he was interested in me, showed me some attention, and paid for the date. Let's just be real for a moment: That takes little effort, if any at all. In fact, that should be a fundamental aspect to a first date, a natural occurrence, not something that shocks you into easy affection. Yes, it was nice! I don't have a problem giving credit where credit is due, but impressive? Well, I wouldn't say so. The problem was that I was so empty and desperate, and due to this social and emotional deficiency, I became oblivious to normalcy when dating. You should never be on the dating scene if you are not strong enough and at least prepared for normalcy, when recovering from an addiction. You don't want to expose yourself too prematurely without understanding the ground rules first.

This is a two-way street; partners should realize the importance of nurturing their relationships so that they are healthy when temptation tries to sneak its way in. Believe me, I don't care who you are or what you look like, temptation does not discriminate. Everyone is subject to temptation. Relationships should be so exhausting with work to preserve and protect it, that the thought of allowing anything, or anyone, to jeopardize it would be an absolute, utmost insult, and not an option.

Back in the Day–My Attempts to Move on

Everything seemed so redundant, and no matter how many different dates I went on, I still could not find happiness. I remember watching the same movie four times in the same month. Each viewing was with a different date, when I finally realized: It was not the men who were wrong, it was me. If it's true that you attract what you are, then how could I possibly attract and offer the best, if I was not my best? At the time, I was broken and resentful. Why would I expose a new person to a bitter woman when this person was not the contributor to my resentment? Why contaminate what could be a potentially successful romantic endeavor? It's just not fair to either party. Your date doesn't deserve it, and you truly can't represent you at your best, under the influence of resentment. If I did not fix the foundation of my problem, which was me, then I simply would continue the cycle of emotional dissatisfaction. I was not well enough to recognize a compatible partner even if he was staring me in the face. I could not recognize him because the deficiency within me tainted my vision and judgment. My accumulated baggage caused me to view new partners the way I viewed my second ex. I grew to expect disrespect and betrayal, even though I hoped for better. I simply was not ready to handle a real man because I was contaminated with nonsense and disconnected from my ability to decipher genuine intentions. The outcome was consistent; I tarnished any new attempt with my desperate chase for love, and the men I did attract simply weren't healthy for me. It was necessary for me to stop and figure out what I was doing and where I was trying to go. It's called self-reflection, where you step outside yourself and see yourself from the outside looking in, to see the full picture of what you are really dealing with. It made perfect sense to me! It took that realization to understand truly what change had to ignite within myself, in order to begin recovery and get my inward beauty and positive outlook on life back.

Awakening to Recovery

In recovery, I became consciously aware of my actions and different desires to include my vices. The adversary had a way of trapping me into my own depression and taking me further then I had anticipated going. While in the stage of depression, I noticed that the things I used to view as morally destructive had become a little more realistic and acceptable. Does that mean they were acceptable? No, it just meant that I had, without realizing, been suppressed into a lifestyle. Had I been strong emotionally, I would have been able to realize that the lifestyle was detrimental to my own well-being. It was at this stage that I understood why so many people had partaken in such immoral behavior, but don't even realize the damnation they were bringing upon themselves, religious or not. It was at that moment that I understood the rationale behind the adages, "Never say never," and "Don't judge a person until you have walked in their shoes." Just because I understand the quotes did not mean that it was okay to behave and feed my immoral addictive tendencies. When I use the word "immoral," I mean anything destructive that prevents you from succeeding as the healthy person you want to be. I'm referring to the balance and peace within you.

I've realized all human beings are vulnerable to addictions, not just the ones trapped in limbo. Because addictions open up avenues to other unwanted potential habits through inadvertence, I understood why many addicts fail in their honest attempt of trying to loosen themselves from the hold that is overwhelmingly strong. I considered myself fortunate because moral values lived inside of me and I did not need an external influence to remind me of my inadequacies. Some addicts are oblivious to their internal conscience and need family and friends to be utilized as the good conscience to convince them into adequacy. Unfortunately, by the time the addiction has surfaced fully, enough for people to recognize it, it's grown to full force and is much more difficult to divorce. There are many destructive obstacles in life that are not necessarily drug induced. That is why this book ties understanding and healing into the breakups or breakaways. If we were striving for emotional success, it completely would be unfair not to obtain such an accomplishment successfully without being educated as to why we are striving for this emotional victory. You don't want to go from broken to healed in one step. Give yourself time to properly dissolve the residue and work through what actually is happening in your life. Where is the accomplishment if you don't allow yourself a chance to understand what's happening? You have to understand the cause of your succumbing to depression, so that you can overcome the many obstacles that will seek to divert your goals, as well as know how to recognize their camouflage. Seriously, do you really think people actually wake up and say, "I want to live a life of depression and addiction?" I don't know about you, but I would venture to say that sane and reasonable people wouldn't want that for themselves. A sane, reasonable person wants happiness. *Sometimes, if you're not careful and smart, happiness is camouflaged by things that only grant temporary satisfaction and long-term destruction.*

I Need Out

I asked myself, how do you get out of such an addictive situation, when the addiction is so strong? Where do you turn when your family and friends have become sick of the same old story over and over again? How do you live with yourself when you know better, but constantly go against your better judgment just to please the satisfaction of your cravings? What is the solution if "LEAVE" doesn't quite comfort your overflow of emotional withdrawal just yet? Distracting the pain is temporary and only exposes the addiction to new areas of your life, which consequentially increases the dose of self-affliction. Covering the pain is even worse because you only ignore the inevitable by prolonging the pain through avoidance. Ridding yourself from the pain by facing it is the only sure cure. Though easier said than done, each option has its pros and cons. The bottom line is that it will not be easy. Otherwise, it could result in one taking so much pain that, by default, enough love is sucked out of you that your body can not start the natural healing process and becomes numb. By then, you may have subjected yourself to permanent damage, or lost valuable time, self-esteem, and more dignity then you would care to admit. At this level, you risk exposing yourself to a world of unwanted demons.

I am well aware that one's emotions and flesh can make relationships that fail feel like a drug that you just can not seem to break away from; thus proving them to be just as addictive as drugs. I decided to take a different approach to the healing process of truly breaking away from an addiction. This form of self-destruction can be the result of failed relationships, drugs, ill thoughts, low self-esteem, and even greed for satisfaction of any sort, resulting in artificial, temporary happiness within. Through my own experience and research, I have

I Need Out—"Motivation of the Author"

documented useful skills and tools, which will be explained further. By utilizing this information, you will be able to learn effectively how to break away from the addiction of unconscious self-destruction.

BENEFITS OF CONQUERING YOUR ADDICTION

In recovering from your addiction, you will start to realize your true value, and things will come to you and unfold like never before. This strong bond of unity, which you will build with yourself from simply conquering such a difficult milestone, will make you feel unstoppable! This feeling is simply the fuel to expose your life to unimaginable dreams. You will uncover the meaning of your existence as formed through your own understanding and not the influence of a parent, grandparent, or friend. This newfound knowledge will awaken you to what you truly want, and the world around you, through clear eyes. This will build such a solid foundation for your new life that nothing will be able to break you down again, unless you allow it. Your confidence will be so strong that even when you walk out of the house lookin' a hot mess, you are still a 10! The reason behind this is because the healing will nurture, and then uncover the confidence that already lives inside of you. Don't misunderstand me now; I am not by any means condoning looking like a hot mess. I am simply saying that you will not rely on your outer appearance to make you who you are; rather, it will enhance what you already have! Those around you will see it and even feel it! People tend to cling to positive energy, and that is exactly what you will exude because you will be healthy. More importantly, this newfound happiness will enable you to:

- Unveil your most creative attributes.
- Build a new life based on the life that is most satisfying to your newfound needs.
- Become pleasant company to be around.
- See the world and the people who live in it as they truly are, and be okay with it.
- Detoxify your way of thinking to positive.
- Allow you to understand the importance of having a plan in life.
- Know when to throw caution to the wind.
- Become wise to the tricks of the adversary.
- Control any ill thoughts and prior addictions that you know will not be conducive to healthy living.
- Become an overall better person.
- Prepare you for the next challenge in life.
- Provide a safety net for your life and those who have been entrusted in your care for the sole purpose of teaching.
- Have a successful relationship by attracting like partners.
- Control anything by letting go of everything!

PREPARING FOR YOUR ROAD TRIP!

As you read along, imagine yourself going on a road trip to a place you never have been before. This road trip will take an indefinite amount of time to complete depending on your sense of direction, positive outlook, determination, and drive. Utilize this book as a map to guide you. Like a map, open your eyes to the dangerous roads, road signs, detours, long routes, short cuts, and most importantly, dead ends. Remember, short cuts are not necessarily the best route to take, as they may have some unforeseen danger you are not prepared to endure. Not to mention that by taking short cuts, you miss out on the important details that may be beneficial to your healing and experience. Don't hinder yourself from a positive experience by taking shortcuts. The goal is to face the deficiency, not avoid it. Prepare and do your research so that you can plan accordingly and not run into unnecessary setbacks. This is your trip, so make the best of it and have an exciting time doing it. The process (and it will be a process) of healing can be fun. Just the anticipation of becoming a better, healthier, and stable person will be enjoyable. It's up to you; you have all the tools you need, if you first believe. While taking this trip, you will come across all types of signs. Some signs will try to distract you; others are merely there to guide you. You will even receive subtle messages that simply are there to remind you that you are on the right track and give you that extra push when you become doubtful.

You already have a head start because you know what direction you are venturing toward, which is to gain control, understanding, and happiness. This knowledge will help you determine how to control your addictions, rid yourself from confusion, and handle the different seasons of life. Allow this journey to flourish through your thoughts as if it was something to live for while detoxifying you into healthy living. Get excited, because once you have finished, you will be a new and improved you, with a better outlook on life and relationships!

Moving on to Chapter 2!

CHAPTER 2

Ready For Change "Setting the Ground Rules"

Understanding Why You are Making the Change

You can not truly break up or break away with any intention that you will return. That is not a breakup, it is a break, and you are merely teaching a lesson to an empty classroom. It's pointless if you know the ultimate cure is to exit. You will have to lose the entitlement you think is owed to you through time, sacrifice, children, money, or anything else if this entitlement is hindering you from moving on with change. *Sometimes, through change, you have to be willing to let go of anything to gain everything.* You have to know when it's simply not worth it, because sometimes entitlements are part of what's holding you back. Trust me when I say that when you are working on doing better for yourself, those old addictive cravings will try to hold you back anyway they can. If you are not willing to let go of it all, whatever you hold on to will be utilized as a new dwelling to keep you captive. Don't give addictive behavior anything to which to attach itself. Let go and welcome change!

You can either change *your* source, or *the* source of the problem; however, the best way to change is by changing *the* source of the problem, which is you. When you attempt to change *your* source, it requires you to depend on someone or something else because *your* source is whatever feeds your addiction, and that is intolerable for you right now. You can not think that changing a person or your addiction will change the problem. The best way for you to change for the better is to change *the* source of the problem, again, which is you. It's about you and your addictive behavior. You cannot afford to depend on anyone, or anything else for your successful healing and recovery, especially if your source has been proven to fail you. If you are truly ready for change, then your focus has to change, and you must change. This effort starts from within because that is where you will determine what is most important for your growth.

Anything worth having is worth working hard for, so understand that with change comes responsibility. When you say you are ready for change, you are saying that you are ready for healing, happiness, wisdom, true love, stability, success, and even hurt. You must realize that you are also accepting that, in order to receive freedom from the force that distracts you from all of these beautiful aforementioned gifts, you will have to fight. Not only will you have to fight through withdrawals and possible confusion, but you will also need to prepare for those difficult and hard times ahead. It's called preparing for your future, similar to preparing your suitcase and first-aid kit for a road trip. As you make this decision to change, there are a few foundational realizations that you must set first in order to properly build an unbreakable you. You have to be able to answer these questions with substantial understanding:

- Why do you want to change?
- Why do you want to break away from your relationship?
- Why do you want to break away from your addiction?
- How will this breakaway change your life?
- What will you learn from this experience?
- What do you want to learn from this experience?
- What kind of growth do you expect from this change?

Remember to look for the good in every situation. When you answer these questions for yourself, answer them with a positive, opened mind set of "I CAN." The answers to the questions will open your eyes to the truth, which may try to slip away from you during recovery when you are faced with justifying your addiction. I can think of a few reasons why I wanted to break away from my past toxic relationship:

- I always was drained emotionally from his behavior.
- I was not being nourished.

- My partner did not believe his actions were a result of my emotional decline, which only continued to inflict more insult to injury.
- I needed recovery, but my partner continued to offer the drug that I was weak to.
- I thirsted for control of my life.
- I was confused in my own mind.
- I wanted life again, and I knew he was not able to understand what that meant; therefore, we could not even attempt to change *together* until he realized this.
- I could not wait any longer; I had to take the lead over my life.
- I craved healing, love, acceptance, and peace within myself.
- I simply wanted to establish everlasting happiness and success without substituting it for temporary satisfaction or a diminished psych.

You have to be real with yourself. This is not a game, and you should not feel as though you have to put on a show for anybody; it's about **you**. Your realizations from reflection will aid you in establishing ground rules for yourself. Yes, I did say ground rules for the self!

I did not set any rules for myself at the beginning of my relationship with my second ex. He was my college sweetheart, and the first guy I dated after moving away from home. I figured, at that time, I was my own woman, which meant that I could do whatever I wanted. What I did not realize was that when I left home, I left with vibrant energy, healthy morals, respect, and discipline. This

Ready For Change—"Setting the Ground Rules"

came from abiding by my mother's rules. I figured her rules were implemented because it was the way she wanted to run her home. Later, I realized it was a way to train my character. She even had restrictions on my food/sugar intake, and this was for my own good, but of course, I did not understand. I remember telling my mom as a kid, right before I got slapped, "I can't wait to be an adult, so I can do whatever I want!" That statement did not sit too well with my mom, but the fact is, many people want the freedom to do whatever they want, not just an eight-year-old kid. I know some adults who wish they did not have restrictions on their time, so they could sleep all day or play video games.

My mom always explained that even though she was an adult, she too had to follow her own rules for herself out of respect. This practice also forced others to respect her as well. Then, as a new adult with all this freedom, I chose to ignore the training. I would visit my ex at any hour of the night and spend the night with him if I did not feel like driving home. I even skipped classes just to be with him if he finished his classes early for the day or had a day off, but he never missed a class to be with me. My lack of discipline was starting to consume my better judgment, and I started sacrificing for him, even though he was not sacrificing for me. He was a senior and did not have the same obligations I had as a freshman. He was a well-seasoned college student, while I was new to college, adulthood, and this found freedom. We had a few classes together and I definitely didn't miss those classes. As you can see, I started this relationship off wrong. I felt that I had no one to answer to, so why not do whatever I felt at the moment? This attitude is what detached me from stability. You always will have someone to answer to, if not to anyone else, then yourself. You don't want to disappoint yourself in the future. You will beat yourself up over it.

Now, detached from stability, tangled into my second ex, and after months of trying to teach him a lesson by breaking up with him for a few days to a week, I moved in with him. I figured his begging validated his assurances never to betray me again, but I was wrong. Again, sound decisions come with discipline. If you train yourself to do exactly what you say you will, it will be natural for you to abide by your own discipline, even if your flesh wants the opposite. However, remember, I forfeited my discipline when I left home after high school and did not continue to respect the purpose of rules. I realized that he had gotten the hang of what to do and say to get me back, and he realized that I'd most likely come back. I was trying to teach him a lesson, but unfortunately I was the only one in the classroom, because he was not concerned with my warnings. He knew that he had me emotionally, and he took advantage of that. I was a slave to my emotions and could not find a way out of the maze. Unsettled by my unhappiness, I forced myself to attempt an exit strategy. I decided to go back to the basics and incorporate my own rules. My first step was moving out of his place and into my own apartment, in an attempt to rebuild myself. It took a little while, but I saved every penny I earned, never losing sight of my goal to move out. Due to my long stretch of undisciplined behavior, it was really hard for me to get back on track. I

Ready For Change—"Setting the Ground Rules"

was used to giving in to whatever I wanted, such as food, sweets, company, TV, laziness, sex, and him. I was damaged goods, fragile, even, but on my way to recovery...or so I thought.

Being ready for change means you have to realize that you may need to give up your current lifestyle if it's not healthy. If you are used to being monogamous and having sex with your partner whenever you feel the urge, then that appetite definitely must be starved. It's not easy at all. If you are not comfortable with being alone, again, you will have to learn to love yourself. In loving yourself, you gain respect and discipline. It's a working effort.

One thing that I did learn, after becoming undisciplined, was that I needed unrestricted access to my own decisions. With that in mind, I hated it when people told me what I could and could not do for the sake of trying to tame me to their liking. I found beauty in originality and being unique in my own way. When I rented my apartment, I did not even have as much as a bed to put in it. However, I had an apartment to call my own, and it was mine, and I was able to begin rebuilding my life based on my desires. It was refreshing that I did not have to depend on anyone to make this move. I had, without realizing it, noticed that it was the beginning of my healing. When I decided to change, I found the door that held the lesson of denying dependency. I did not even know how to get an apartment, or what was needed in order to have my own place. My desire and drive opened my curiosity; that then pushed me to finding out how. After I sought and met all of the requirements, I successfully moved into this new chapter of my life, all by myself. It was the first time I ever had lived by myself. I was independently making decisions based on my needs for a healthier life. It's amazing how things miraculously unfold when you are doing what is right.

After moving in to my apartment, I made quite a few rules for myself. Some were really hard, while others were very easy to abide. I basically was creating balance for myself by preparing for my future through what I already knew would be my own kryptonite. I designed my rules in this way so that I always could have something to reach for and destroy any feelings of doubt through discouragement, just in case I broke any of my own rules. No one is perfect, so if you make rules for yourself and then break them, don't be discouraged or give up; just know that perfect practice eventually makes perfect. Always work towards perfection and never give up, but *hold yourself accountable*. There were consequences if I broke my rules. That's how I held myself accountable. The easy rules were basically there for encouragement and structure. If I could follow the easy rules, then I knew I could do anything. We are not perfect beings. I knew I was not exempt from failure, but my desire to succeed had to overpower the subjection to failure. Below are a few suggestions, as these were the rules that I had set for myself.

Difficult Rules:
- No verbal, physical, or electronic contact with my ex for six months.
- No thinking about the situation that broke us up for longer than five minutes.

Ready For Change—"Setting the Ground Rules"

- No reminiscing about our good times.
- No wallowing in grief by listening to songs or looking at photos that reminded me of my ex.
- No justifying how we can get back together.
- No talking about the situation until I am able to handle the pain.
- No going back!

The last one was really hard. He was my addiction-companion and I craved him.

Easy Rules

- No personal phone calls from any romantic interest past 8 p.m.
- Proclaim healing over my emotions at least once a week by reflecting on myself with quiet time.
- Replace any negative energy or thoughts to positive energy and thoughts.
- Keep my outer appearance beautiful, even if the inside feels lifeless when I walk out of the house.
- Compliment *myself* at least twice a day.
- Once every two weeks, take *myself* on a date and have fun.
- If I give in to my addiction, remind myself that I am always in control and that this weakness is only temporary.

You don't have to follow my same rules; it's just an example of what worked for me. If you decide to make rules for yourself, make a set of rules that you know you can abide by, and some that may be difficult, but well worth it if accomplished. My suggestion would be to make a list of reprimands based on which rules were broken in order to hold yourself accountable to your change. If I were to break one of my easy rules I would pull a more strict punishment than I would if I had broken a difficult rule. There was absolutely no reason for me to break an easy rule, and if I did, it was a sure sign I was disrespecting myself, which was unacceptable. Set consequences that will force you to not want to break your own rules. Most importantly, understand the severity of setting order and boundaries to your life. It is so easy to give up and say, "I don't want or have to do this," but the bottom line is that in order to have a successful, vibrant life, you must have discipline, balance, and order. That is true in everything you do. Below were the things I did to hold myself accountable. If I had broken a rule from the difficult rules list, these were my consequences:

Difficult Broken Rules:

- Two hours of quiet, uninterrupted, deep meditation during primetime for one week.
- Three days of classical music only, if I listened to any music at all (I chose to turn off the radio).
- One week of water and green tea only as beverages.
- Go to bed one hour early and wake up one hour early every day for two weeks.

Ready For Change—"Setting the Ground Rules"

If I had broken a rule from the easy rules list, my consequences were a little different; see below:

Easy Broken Rules

- No cell phone privileges for a week (I turned the phone OFF and left it in the closet, even on the weekends).
- No sweets for a week.
- No watching my favorite TV shows.
- Retract personal phone call privileges for three days.
- Cardio exercise three days out of the week for a one-hour duration.
- All of this plus the difficult broken rules list.

Mystery Behind the Rules

If you will notice, all of my rules, as well as consequences, were all tied into healing and eventually worked to my benefit. I had surrounded myself, even if I fell short and gave in, with healing, recovery, reflection, meditation, and exercising control, even over my personal space and social life. Aside from friends and family, this inward healing was my support system. The purpose of retracting phone privileges and the deep meditations were to force me to learn how to depend on myself for relief and not rely on others for sole assistance. I needed to master being alone before I was ready to handle any outside interventions. I had to familiarize myself with being alone and make it normal. It was the only way to feel comfortable in my new life and my new state of being without a constant companion. Activities focusing on meditation, breathing, and relaxation especially were helpful with combating anxiety and stress.

Retracting sweets worked as a dual enhancement. It allowed me to control something that I loved so much by restricting my intake, and was also healthy for my body. I found that when I consumed a lot of unhealthy foods, such as sweets, it weighed me down physically; I had no energy. That did not help at all when I already was drained emotionally. Avoiding primetime TV as one of my punishments allowed me more time to focus on my goals, undistracted. I did not feel primetime television was productive to my healing, and I did not want the TV to be used as an idle pleasure. The whole purpose of this healing was to really get a better understanding of myself while practicing control and learning discipline again.

Exercising provided multiple enhancements because physical activity is known to reduce depression, anxiety, and improve your mood. I learned that intense training or moderate aerobic workouts increase the levels of chemicals in the brain such as adrenaline, endorphins, serotonin, and dopamine. These chemicals produce feelings of pleasure and empowerment after working out. According to researchers, when you are depressed, these chemicals are lowered, which explains why we tend to feel devoured and weak when life seems to be upside down. Exercising instantly can turn these levels, right side up. I guess that explains why I was "so excited," and had a heightened feeling of "freedom from the relationship" after working out. I even found that it enhanced my creativity, imagination, and physically transformed my outer appearance. At such an emotional time of your life, you need to feel confident and pleased with how you look and with simply being you. Complimenting myself everyday added positivity into the universe, even if I didn't feel positive at the time. I made myself speak those words into existence because I believe words are very powerful. Why not speak positivity into your life?

ABIDING BY THE RULES

Take a moment and think about why rules are established everywhere you go. This should start from home. Your parents or guardians, as authority figures, are supposed to provide you with your first training of discipline. They set rules to mold and discipline us in order to prepare us for the real world and society. This preparation should provide foundational structure in order to get us through the many levels of life. Then, we go to school. There are also rules set in place to discipline us in scholastic/social civilization, sort of like a discipline of the mind in order to take us to yet another level in life. Next are the local laws within each city, which are enforced to maintain and coordinate mass structure. Without structure, there would be chaos; this is ultimately the case for us as individuals. Rules are simply a form of respect. We don't have to give respect, and we don't have to follow the rules, but there are consequences if we choose to be undisciplined by disobeying rules and denying respect, even for ourselves. The repercussions can result in untamed behavior like clinging to addictions or toxic relationships. Understand that the only thing we truly own and control in this life is our self and the actions we choose to make. It would be in our highest interest to heed awareness of discipline and control.

Think about your training as a child. If you had an authority figure that set rules in order to provide you discipline, then you had a great start to life. As a child, and in an environment where rules are enforced, if the rules were disregarded, it's normal to assume you would be punished and chastised somehow, by getting whipped, grounded, or having your privileges taken away. You only hurt yourself through defiance. As you get older, the training you learned from home should be exercised in school. If you don't exercise good home training and you break the rules at school, you are suspended or ordered to go to detention of some sort, and some schools still paddle or expel indefinitely. Moving past home and school rules brings us to the rules in the local cities in which we live. If we break local city laws, we pay fines, are summoned to perform community service, and, in extreme cases, lose our freedom to jail; sort of like losing your control and forfeiting free will to something or someone else. It's all about control over self. After all, that is what discipline is, right? Do you see the similarities to all of the consequences? It seems to me that they all fall back to reflecting on yourself, because parents/guardians ground, schools detain, and cities jail; all of which will force you to go back to your own foundation, the ground, which should have been built from home

Ready For Change—"Setting the Ground Rules"

as a child. Look up the word "grounded" for yourself. You will find that it suggests a sort of fundamental aspect to structure. It's that simple! Understand that this whole respect and rule illustration goes far beyond home, school, and city. There is a huge universe out there. I'm referring to the grand scheme of things. It's the fundamental skills that will afford each of us the opportunity for growth, but its starts from within.

Have you ever been to church or a doctor's appointment, a friend's house, or a school function, and saw a chaotic, disrespectful child that was completely out of line right in front of the parent? What is the first thing to strike your thoughts? Let me help you out a little bit. Perhaps you shake your head in disbelief while thinking to yourself "what a shame, that kid needs:"

- A whippin'.
- Discipline.
- To be locked away.
- To be put in his/her place and realize who's the adult.
- Medication.
- Love and attention.

I can go on and on about what you may be thinking about this child, not to mention what you may think of the guardian. All of those thoughts may be true. However, when I see a child like that, I also think to myself, with compassion, that this poor kid probably has some type of disability, or has not been exposed to the first level of fundamental structure. My heart goes out to that child. Just like you can spot dysfunctional homes in a classroom by a child's behavior, the same is evident in the prisons all around the world full of individuals who lack respect or control for "IT" and clearly didn't exercise fundamental structure. You may ponder, what is "IT?" Well, "IT" can be whatever you may disrespect, to include your own personal rules, or "IT" could mean Individual Training. I cannot stress enough how such things start from within.

There are several stages to life that are simply prerequisites, designed to successfully carry us to the next level of life. If you do not secure success in each level, you are destined for difficulty in the future. Some even may find themselves wanting to go back to a level, which may now be deemed puerile to their current stage in life. This is the case for individuals who have either grown up too fast, vainly passing through the vital stages of life, or simply lack proper training. I'd like to call it immature behavior. Don't skip levels or take what you think is the easy way out. You owe it to yourself to live life through the good and bad times.

Some may have a great understanding of respect and control, while many may not. You have to set rules for yourself in order to solidify your personal foundation. This foundation is vital to your success, because just like home, school, and city rules are designed to mold proper discipline and structure, so will your rules be for yourself. You need to know exactly what you will and will not accept, and stick to it. You have to cement your rules in your foundation so that they will not change by the forces of the wind or flesh.

Ready For Change—"Setting the Ground Rules"

Your foundation of rules will act as your point of origin. You may even find yourself passing your techniques to your next generation. Whatever works for you should surly entice your offspring, as they are merely an extension of you. Perhaps, your vices may complicate them as well. Therefore, why not give them a head start to what worked for you? Forming a foundation is planning for the future, so be sure to make it worthwhile. You just may have to fall back on it during tough times. You get out what you put in, and you always reap what you sow. Don't look at your rules as a way of depriving yourself. Instead, view them as a way of respecting yourself and gaining control. Others will be forced to respect you as well, and so will your addiction. You even will start to become aware of nonsense when you spot instances that try to pull you further from your achievement. It is always your choice, and your choices always will affect you.

If you master respect and control, you will solidify a concrete foundation in your healing process. It starts from within!

MISERY & ALONENESS

While preparing for change, we must also be aware of the camouflage of depression and not slip into its trap. Breaking away from addictions often can feel like a lonely progression. Choosing to be alone is a very hard task to overcome; in fact, some totally deny that true aloneness can act as a cure to pain. Reflecting on the self through being alone brings awareness to the insecurities that you might have been feeling. Through that awareness, you are able to target the healing. There truly isn't anything wrong with spending time with yourself and getting to know who you truly are. It's actually quite invigorating. It will be difficult at first, but remember, we are already prepared for difficulty. It even has its own zipper in the suitcase, so embrace it.

Remember, misery loves company. Therefore, don't get caught up with anything or any thoughts that will encourage misery and discourage progress, such as wasting valuable time on trying to figure out why you are not good enough. Add this to the foundation that you are building:

> *As long as you have the breath of life flowing through your body, you are worth it to you, and you are more than good enough for anything. You do not need an audience to reassure you of that.*

Why spend each night crying or feeling uneasy because you are afraid of being alone or wishing for someone else to change? Why remain intimate, while at the same time hoping to get back what you are giving? This behavior only will postpone the inevitable. Instead, cry because you are happy that you learned how to let go of depending on someone or something else to make you happy. Overjoy your emotions because now everything you once gave will be returned to you. Realize that you do not have to give your time and energy to someone or something that does not deserve it. Literally treat yourself like deserving royalty. I mean it. Turn that love around to yourself. You must face the truth and your fears because it is not until then that this nightmare will be over. Do not choose misery because you do not want to be lonely or you want a safety net to fall back into, just in case the loneliness is too overwhelming. You have to determine what is really keeping you captive. When you say that you are ready for change, you accept that it will not be easy. So, by all means prepare for this distraction. Where does it start? That is right, from within. Get excited because you are building the masterpiece to your life. True love knows when to let go. Remember, in order to gain it all you must be willing to let it all go.

Accepting that You are Going to Hurt

One cold rainy night, while sitting in the living room of my empty apartment, thunder struck and out went the electricity. I opened the blinds to invite some of the streetlights in to shine in my pitch-black apartment. The wind was blowing, and all I could see, from three stories high, were the tops of cars in the parking lot of my complex. Inside my apartment was dead silence, which accentuated the sound of the wind and rain hitting the rooftop. After an hour or so had passed, I began to feel scared, but I didn't know why. This was the first time I had to face my pain one-on-one since I had moved out. During the move, I used my adrenaline from getting my very own apartment and the excitement of change to distract my hurtful feelings of breaking away. I was so excited that I forgot about all the pain I would have to face after I actually was settled in, and was alone in my apartment. In that moment of solitude, I entertained the feeling of doubt. I started feeling the discomfort and pressure of time versus healing. All I could think of was how long I had to travel to get where I was trying to go. In my mind, I didn't know how long I would have to feel this way before I found comfort. I decided to reach out to my family on my cell phone. I trusted my family to act as a road sign in my time of doubt and to encourage me by assuring me I was going the right way and to keep going. I was only able to contact my brother, Adonis, and he gave me the best advice to keep me fueled in the right direction. Due to the pain and withdrawal I was experiencing at that moment, I was able to relate to his message; otherwise it would have been like a riddle I could not understand. He told me not to be weak, and to understand that it's going to hurt, so persevere. I was able to relate, because I was at war with the pain that I needed to overcome. I fought the painful energy with discipline. I told myself that I was stronger than the pain and that I would not allow it to break me, because I was fighting for a purpose. I put in my mind that, by enduring it, I would allow the pain to make me stronger. I could not afford for this type of hindrance to haunt me later in life. This was a real internal battle; I was on the front line facing my own internal demons.

    Many people deny the fact that breaking away from something that consumes your whole being is physically painful to let go of. Think about it: You may not be able to see the feeling that the addictions give you, but you feel it. How can anyone explain what they have never seen? You only go by what you feel. If you happen

Ready For Change—"Setting the Ground Rules"

to fall in the category of people that are in denial, do not cancel out the possibility that your pain *can* be *addressed* and *faced* head on because you can not actually see it. There are plenty of things around us, even now, that we can not see, and it could be standing right in front of us. How about the fact that you are best friends with the addiction that is working to destroy you? Is your enemy not right in your face, but perhaps in a different form? I am familiar with the quote, "Keep your friends close and your enemies closer," but you can not lose yourself to the enemy; otherwise, you defeat the purpose of that quote. You should not get comfortable with having no control. Even though sometimes you can not physically see the infliction of hurt, you feel it when you are stripped away from your addiction because it is now a part of you. Our bodies were made to live and heal themselves when pain is inflicted or withdrawal consumes us. So, approach hurt with delight, because that is a sign to let you know your body is working properly.

If you are hurting, then you are healing. The time to be concerned is when you are numb and feel nothing, because you will have hurt to look forward to. You have to experience the hurt or withdrawal in order to rid yourself of toxins and get better. Hurting is the first stage to recovery and healing. It is our natural makeup. We were created with a natural healer within. If you feel as though you are disconnected from your natural healer, you will have to get away from worldly distractions in order to find it. Worldly pleasures bring about distractions and lead you further from the truth. Prepare yourself for the inevitable obstacles.

Understanding Your Body

The moment we began living was the moment our bodies began fighting to stay alive. When oxygen filled our lungs and life was given to our bodies, we began living as we know it today in this universe. We are made up of so many undiscovered, intricate mechanisms, that even today, after over 200,000 years of scientifically walking the Earth, human beings have yet to be fully understood or mastered. However, what is undoubtedly known is that after life was given, we were designed to live because our bodies were designed to heal themselves. It is natural for the body to feel when something is wrong and then automatically begin a healing process to cure the discomfort. For instance, if you cut yourself, it heals naturally, unless the natural process is aborted deliberately. Once the brain realizes something is wrong, it sends chemical signals to heal the wound. I believe this illustration can work for the heart, mind, body, and soul if we yield awareness to its function. In order to heal properly, we must first allow our natural healers to begin the recovery process to our strife.

When we want to learn how something works normally, we study and research its function for complete understanding, until we are satisfied with our familiarity. In essence, this particular subject consumes our interest and time. After we have understood the objectives, it becomes easier to relate to its functions and even could become second nature to our everyday activities. When you master something so well that it becomes second nature to you, it is easier to problem solve and realize a solution if issues arise and

Ready For Change—"Setting the Ground Rules"

interrupt normal functions. If you do not understand how or why something operates the way it does, it would be next to impossible to repair it properly if damaged. There is a cause and effect to everything, which leads me into the next topic.

Take for instance, blood types. If you know your blood type, you can research many things to help you understand how to combat many of your emotional feelings. I always knew my blood type, but I never knew what it meant, or how it affected me individually. Because I was in search of learning how I functioned as an individual, I researched some things about me that doctors naturally would have exposed me to. After all, the inside of me was what I was trying to heal, anyway. In the book "Eat right 4 Your Type," Dr. Peter J. D'Adamo explains that our blood type is one of the keys to unlocking the door to the mysteries of emotional strength, disease, health, and physical vitality. Dr. Peter further explained how our blood type can determine our susceptibility to illness, which foods we should eat, and how we should exercise. He found that our blood type factored in our energy levels, emotional responses to stress, and perhaps even in our personality. It is no wonder that certain foods and medicines affect individuals differently. If you do not know what is best for your body, how can you know what is best for you? How awesome would it be to just eat an apple and have all emotional pains vanish? Though contrary, it does have some truth. If we take the time out to learn more about the way we operate and the reason why certain things affect our bodies, mood swings, or cravings, then perhaps half the battle of addictive behavior would be won. Take the time out and learn who you truly are from the inside out.

Crying is the Best Gift of Healing

I've run across some people who purposely have avoided crying because they felt it was a sign of weakness. In many countries that may very well be the case, but I do not agree with that at all. I never feel ashamed to release pain, hurt, or anxiety through tears, because tears are one of our natural healers. We were made with three different types of tears: basal, reflex, and psychic or emotional tears. The basal tears lubricate our eyes so that we can see properly without discomfort, while the reflex tears are produced if the eyes become irritated or poked. It is scientifically proven that, of the three different types of tears, the psychic or emotional tears are designed as a natural painkiller to heal emotional discomfort and stress. I like to call them the "healing" tears, because they trigger chemicals in the brain that promote protein-based hormones, for the sole purpose of ridding the body of emotional pollutants. Many believe that the body, in times of emotional stress, depends on this gland to release excess amounts of chemicals and hormones, in order to return it to a balanced level. It is amazing that we all were designed with healing tears to comfort our inevitable pain. So, again, do not be ashamed of crying, because when you cry from withdrawal, you are healing your discomfort. You should welcome tears of healing. I actually exercise this gift to balance my feelings, in an effort to gain control. The best advantage to this natural pain killer is that it has no side effect. Think about this when the distraction of manmade drugs tempts you into easing your pain. Drugs *temporarily* allow you to feel better or help to avoid the real problem, while the disease continues to get worse. You can cure yourself once you stop doing the things that provoke the disease and/or addiction. You already have the painkiller, and it is within. So cry it out!

Prepare for Distractions

I believe that there is a force out there that does not want us to have control, thus holding us as slaves to addictions and captivity. If you agree to change, then you should open your eyes to the force of distraction, in order to prepare yourself to overpower its will. Distractions divide attention from your goal through procrastination and often times come in the form of confusion; this is why I stress that it is vital to build a healthy and concrete foundation in your healing. You need to build a foundation that you can trust in times of confusion. If ever you become distracted through confusion or temptation, you will not get lost if you plant the truth within your foundational plan. Allow this truth to guide you to success. If, along the way, things around you do not seem to agree and you do not feel quite right, you will have to trust that your foundation is the truth. You will have to revert to your map quite frequently along the way. Be sure to plan in advance and start building a strong foundation.

Distractions can be inflicted or afflicted. If the distractions are inflicted, that would mean something, or someone else is the tempter. Afflicted distractions are either conscious or unconscious distractions that you put on yourself, which means you are the tempter. Don't get caught up. Leave the unnecessary baggage behind, and do not try to squeeze in something that simply does not fit or belong. This form of behavior is only an extension of demise. It is similar to when I knew my second ex was not going to treat me as I needed to be treated, and yet I found and justified a reason to go back. Pay attention to what you are doing and where you are trying to go. Depression has a way of sucking you into distractions, especially when you are focused and doing well. You can recognize it by reverting to your foundation of rules. If it is not on your rule list, or it breaks any of your rules, it is simply a distraction. With growth, you will begin to feel and discern when something is not right, but you have to be in tune with yourself. Give it some time, you will get there; trust and believe.

The main obstacle, which you want to understand and overcome, through recognition, is the act of assisting distractions in the name of depression. Don't assist distractions. Make that one of your rules. After you have made the decision to change, you will realize that the next stage in the healing process is hurt and withdrawal before you find contentment. In this stage, it is very easy to become discouraged by giving into depression. If you give into your depression, all you will have to look forward to is hurt, and lots of

Ready For Change—"Setting the Ground Rules"

it. Don't get caught up in the details, you have to look at the bigger picture. Yes, you will hurt, but it will not last forever; in fact, as each new experience consumes your mind, the hurt eventually will subside, and then disappear. It is like pouring water into a glass of red Kool-Aid. If you continue to fill the glass with water, eventually all of the impurities will spill out and the contents will become clear again. You can not give up, and you definitely can not add more Kool-Aid to the glass if the goal is to clear the substance. As long as you remember your goal, you will not be distracted as easily unless you choose to be.

Instead, take advantage of conscious and unconscious awareness and keep a positive outlook about this exciting endeavor to change. You have your whole life ahead of you, so endure a little to gain a lot. No pain, no gain! Get excited about the outcome and profess your excitement now. It's only going to get better if you continue healing, I promise you. By the time you finish recovery, you will look back on your life as a wiser person and say to yourself, "What took me so long?"

In the same way that you have to watch out for distractions, you must also be vigilant to how they can seep into to your environment via negative thoughts, negative speaking, and negative actions. During your recovery, you need only to pour positivity into your healing process. Monitor what you think and speak into the universe. Try it for three days. The next three days, spend time alone, but fill your schedule. Tell yourself that you are healed, you are happy, and that life is beautiful! Most importantly, believe it!

Treat yourself and cater to this feeling that you have proclaimed, and see what happens to you in the next three days! You have to make it happen. I would suggest turning down any potential candidates; this is **your** time. Make an attempt to smile during the next three days. No frowning or sadness, even if it means your cheeks start aching from your constant smiling. You want people to believe you are elated because they will treat you as such. Who knows, even if you don't feel it, you just may become what you proclaim, because like attracts like.

Below are a few suggestions of how you can book your schedule for the next three days to avoid and deny distractions:

Day 1: Rent three funny movies. If you are low on cash, then go to the public library; it's free! Try watching them all back to back!

Day 2: Schedule a day of **window-shopping**. Only look at items that will help to brighten your day.

Note of Advice

STOP! Don't buy anything! We don't want to make you out to be an emotional spender/shopper. That will only make for other unwanted depressions, like debt or clutter.

Day 3: Go out and do three things to change your appearance, or you can do something you never have done before. This can sort of be an initiation to your new beginning.

Ready For Change—"Setting the Ground Rules"

For example, test drive a new car, get a wig, go to the back of your closet and put on the outfit you forgot you even had, or change your lipstick color. It has to be something that will ignite a feeling of something different.

GET FED UP!

There is a difference between having the stamina of a true, loyal, "do or die" person to something you stand by, and being too hopeful and wasting your time on something that is just not going to make you a better person at the end of the day. During my struggles, I felt as though my commitment to love and remaining loyal meant that I had to remain in my unhealthy relationships, even though my partners were killing me emotionally. The truth of the matter was that my partners did not deserve the kind of love and commitment I was lavishing upon them, because they did not respect it. In essence, by thinking that I had to remain true and loyal to my partners, who were helping to destroy my life, I actually betrayed the love I needed for myself. Revisit why you are being so loyal and you will find out if it is due to your insecurities or if the addiction has imprisoned your judgment. When I use the phrase "do or die," I'm referring to someone who is so loyal that, no matter what happens, they hold true to their loyalty. A true "do or die" person's character is unique because they are disciplined, and they know when to commit their loyalty to such worthiness. They also can recognize impersonators, those that pretend to be worthy of this type of commitment. If deep down inside, you know your addiction is not worthy of your commitment, then "get fed up," and prepare for yourself to break away and heal.

    I have met many people, both men and women, including myself, who admitted that they simply were not fed up yet, and so they stayed in their toxic relationship that always seemed to get worse. They were not ready to move on, because they did not know how to prepare themselves for detachment. In my case, sometimes I just did not want to face the pain I would have to endure. The best way to encourage change is to get fed up. You can do this several ways. As mentioned before, laying a solid foundation will allow you to know what you will or will not put up with. You have to make sure you know what you want and what you believe in, in order to have something to stand by. Therefore, if you are unhappy, then direct your goals towards finding happiness. It is that simple. You can do this by setting a goal for what you want, and then set a time frame in which you demand it. Keep in mind that in order to establish your own sense of boundaries, you will have to have a threshold. Enforcing your happiness and goals will allow you to get fed up. You have to have a limit on how low you will stoop. Without a limit, how would you know when you have hit the bottom? It is important to know when you have reached the bottom line. Once you have gotten there, there is no more going lower, and it is time to make a change towards the other direction. I understand that sometimes we tend to lower our standards and accept things we normally would not accept because we have made mistakes of our own. Perhaps those mistakes made us feel that maybe we deserve to be treated unfavorably, to even the score of disrespect. Just remember, *you have to be your best if you want to receive the best.* Do not utilize your past mistakes as an excuse for subjecting yourself to less than the best. Heed the Golden Rule: Do unto others as you would have them do unto you. This way you always will act with integrity, and this in turn will allow you to expect and demand it in return.

It is very important to confirm your threshold of "enough is enough," because if you don't, you will continue to decline emotionally, mentally, and physically. Don't ever get comfortable in an unhealthy relationship or addiction, because sooner or later, it will attack you. Maintaining happiness is important to humanity because the body is one unit of energy. If one part of you attracts unhappiness, your whole body will feel it, and so will the people and world around you. People even will begin to treat you in a way that would be in agreement to how you feel. Therefore, right now, right here, appoint your threshold and say enough is enough. Take charge! Get fed up and take control of your life! That is what change is all about; taking control of your life means submerging yourself in what you strive to be like.

Quest for Revenge

One late evening, I became so angry at the way my second ex disregarded my feelings and simply did whatever he wanted to do, with whomever he wanted to do it. This particular night, I had reached my threshold of bullshit, and it was time to let it all out. I had so much rage and anger in my heart for him. In the heat of the argument I screamed, "I wish you were dead," and it didn't move him one bit. After realizing my words did not move him, I charged at him as if I really was going to do some damage. Caught up in my adrenaline, I actually was convinced that I would hurt him. I stood at 5' 2", 135 lbs., while he stood 5' 11" at 180 lbs., and do I have to mention the fact that he was a **man**? Naturally, if he were the type of man to hit a woman, I would have had the daylights knocked out of me that night. I wanted to kill him in the heat of my emotional disaster. I grew even angrier because I had no control of my situation; he was controlling my emotions through his actions, or lack thereof. I thought, for a split second, if I could do something to hurt him, then maybe then he would feel how I felt. He simply held me, and all of my rage, so tight that I could barely breathe, and said, "You need to calm down; otherwise, I will have you arrested." I thought, the nerve of him to even go that far, and it made me even angrier. He had no idea his lack of caring was provoking my rage.

I screamed from the pit of my soul, "I can't breathe!" I felt claustrophobic and helpless all at the same time because he was not letting up. Through the struggle, he ended up sitting on me and managed to get a few scratches that later were used to my advantage. Needless to say, he called the police on me and wanted me to go to jail. Once the police arrived, their expressions appeared to be that of shock for I guess two reasons: One, his apartment looked as though a tornado had gone through it, and two, my ex, "a man,"

Ready For Change—"Setting the Ground Rules"

was the one that called in the disturbance. By the time the police arrived, we both had decided that neither of us was leaving. The heat had simmered, and our pride was the only thing holding on to what had happened. He told the police to take me to jail as if they were the mediator of our fight and jail was not serious. I just did not care at that point. The police took me outside, where they saw all of my bruises from the struggle and figured we were hitting each other and gave us a choice: Either we both go to jail, or no one goes to jail. Needless to say, neither one of us spent the night in jail that night, but he sure was angry that I hadn't gone to jail. My rage sought revenge, and I almost went to jail for it. How would I explain to my family that I was in jail and needed someone to bail me out? I had never been in trouble with the law before. This goes to show you that revenge will get you nowhere.

Just like good and bad, righteousness and evil, positive and negative, distractions also can creep in while you are getting fed up. Don't let them! Stay on the positive road to success. Know that revenge is not what "getting fed up" is all about. I repeat, do not quest for revenge in order to get fed up. Revenge is a direct trick and distraction of a negative force. We are not on a vengeance quest. We are in the frequency of healing through positive control. In the words of my dad, "If you are right, then stay right." You will be rewarded for your obedience. It is so easy to slip into hate from love; after all, if you did not love, then you could not hate. Love is good/righteous/positive energy, and hate is bad/evil/negative energy. You have to care enough about something in order to desire something as strong as hate; otherwise, you would not care to hate it. There is a thin line between love and hate. Guess what? The common cure for hate is love. Therefore, don't give in to revenge by exerting negative energy on vengeance, because you will reap what you sow, and it will come back to you. In an effort to revolve love around you, sow love so that you can grow an abundance of righteous fruits. Don't worry about whatever doesn't grow, because it was dead anyway, and you did not need it to succeed. Don't feel discouraged when you plant something that does not grow. You can never have too much love. I have learned the best revenge is letting go and never looking back. If you happen to find yourself looking backwards, that just may be the direction you are traveling. Stay focused on your goal, and continue to move forward.

Understanding how You Became Addicted

Think back to what caused your addiction. What caused the overflow of desire, resulting in the loss of control by losing balance? Why were you curious? What knowledge did you lack? What was the tempter, and did you know you would like it that much? Have you ever observed someone who shared the same weakness as you? You knew exactly where they would fall short, because you were quite familiar with their kind. You could tell what they would do next after being exposed to the weaknesses' force. You were able to predict this based off what you knew about the force. Perhaps, had someone been there to pre-inform you, you might have been able

Ready For Change—"Setting the Ground Rules"

to balance or even avoid what you now may not be able to resist. How would you know that crack/cocaine was addictive, if no one told you? How would you know that physical infatuation is simply your brain on a natural drug similar to speed, which makes you feel overly fascinated about a person, if no one ever told you? How could you possibly know about the detriment of addictions if you never were informed? Life would be so much clearer if we could identify our point of origin, and by that I do not just mean Mom and Dad. The lack of knowing where you came from coupled with a lack of historical information is like reinventing the wheel and setting yourself up for a lot of unnecessary mistakes.

Before you can agree to change, or understand where you are going, it is very wise to know where you came from to avoid getting lost. This is also true when identifying what attracted you to the addiction or why you lost control in the first place. Many people are like magnets, and can not understand why they continue to attract their weakness. There is a reason for this, and learning why would allow you to redirect your focus. It even will expose you to the subtle answers, which will help to form your own positive conclusion. Everything and everyone has a point of origin. Understanding where you came from can assist you in finding the answers to why you are made the way you are. For example, let us use family as an illustration. You truly can learn a great deal about yourself by studying your own family. They carry all of your strengths, weakness, and even DNA. We tend to better identify with familiarity as opposed to things we do not understand. It is a natural instinct, which is why you can understand yourself by observing your family. You may notice that one of your family members' weaknesses may be your strength. Therefore, you grow wiser by understanding the results of that weakness before ever experiencing it or traveling down the road. In this case, you optimize your strengths through repetition, because you know better than to do the opposite. The opposite also could be true, their strength could be your weakness, and now you have something to strive for, because you know what you could mature into if you just controlled the weakness. Overall, you get a better understanding of what to look out for and what will harm you through the history of understanding your background. There is no need to reinvent the wheel if you do not have to.

Face your weaknesses and capitalize on your strengths. We all have weaknesses. Recognizing your weaknesses will teach you how to resist and not be haunted by them. You can obtain this form of structure by being honest with yourself. Make a list of all the forces that you battle with and why. Think about how you felt before you lost control and did not depend on your addiction for happiness. Preparing for change means you will have to get ready to sort out your demons.

In the same way you learn about yourself from observing family, you also can learn a great deal by researching your internal makeup. Spend time getting to know how and why you function the way you do. The main goal here is to get an understanding of **you** so that you can know where you are going and not drive blindly on cruise control.

Ready For Change—"Setting the Ground Rules"

Last, but not least, don't get comfortable in an unhealthy relationship or circumstance. If you have understood the adage "birds of a feather flock together," then you can relate to why this advice is vital. Our environment, the people we hang around, and our daily circumstances influence our focus and tend to change us. When you submerge your time in repetitive occurrences, they naturally become a part of you. Either you will change, or the person around you will change, depending on who is more dominant. Rest assured that someone will change. You can not hang around the same person comfortably and not expect something to change if the two of you are different. In order to become fluent at what you want, you have to somewhat lose yourself in the indulgence, but always maintain control for versatility and so that you don't get lost. If you get comfortable in an unhealthy relationship, you only diminish the way you see yourself. You will inevitably stunt your self-esteem, and ultimately become a threat to your own growth. This behavior results in the downward spiral to self-destruction, and you will find yourself doing things you once despised.

FINAL PREPARATION FOR THE ROAD AHEAD

Now that I have prepped you for change, are you still ready to take that step? I don't expect any other answer but **yes!** Look at your preparation as a way to form a new foundation for your brand new life. You have to be honest with yourself and realize what you are going through. Obstacles are a purposefully posed adversary to diminish growth and will always be there to stifle growth. Once you realize those obstacles are there to set you back, then you can properly prepare for the challenges you will have to overcome. Account for the obstacles in your preparations to keep them from diverting progress.

You have to be ready! Only you can understand your plight and learn from the sting to make the best recovery for yourself. It is not wise to deny yourself the experience of heartache. It is the experience that will sustain your decisions and teach growth. Never feel stupid, or that you are wasting your time, because whatever happiness is to you will keep you through. It is the experience that will help you to stay on the right track. Nobody can tell you when enough is enough, except **you!** Determine what enough is and embrace your experience, good or bad, in order to optimize your recovery and map your route to freedom. Staying true to you means valuing your self-worth and life. Life should be lived in happiness and truth, not agony and deceit.

Remember, the first step in building anything is laying a solid foundation. Your foundation is vital to your development because it keeps you stable. When you are ready to embark upon change, begin building your foundation with strategic thought. Your progress is up to you. Take into account what you want and what you are ready to handle right now. This is a building process, and you have to start from somewhere. The cure for your pain is love. Love yourself through continuous healing.

Ready For Change—"Setting the Ground Rules"

Remember the tools you will need in order to build a solid foundation and visualize your checklist as a guide.

Recollect the checklist:

- Know why you are making the change.
- Know your point of origin.
- Set goals as guidance on how you will accomplish change.
- Set rules and hold yourself accountable.
- Accept that you are going to hurt.
- Cry as much as you can.
- Get fed up, if you are not already.
- Stay away from revenge.
- Prepare for distractions.
- Do not misconstrue aloneness as misery.
- Understand your background.
- Love through continuous healing.

Now that we have the checklist finished, enjoy your trip to healing and revert to your foundation if ever you feel a little detached from reality. It is this foundation that will stabilize your new energy to healing and the truth. It starts from within.

Two chapters down,
...and on to Chapter 3
You can do it!
You're almost there...
Total Independence

CHAPTER 3

Detoxifying Your Focus

Focus

I've strongly emphasized the importance of understanding what all goes into change, in order to prepare you for the road ahead. Assuming you have decided to take this route, you will have to allow yourself a chance to heal, by mentally detoxing from your past and guarding what you think, say, and do. Guarding your mind and actions can be very difficult at first because it is easy to slip back into old habits if your focus has not gone through mental detoxification. The smallest infraction, such as the frustration from denying yourself the pleasure of what you are trying to resist, can bring you right back into the old habits of your addiction. It all stems from a lack of disciplining yourself to say "**no**" to fickle desires. Your partner was a part of you, which makes it natural for you to undergo withdrawal after separation, because you are mentally detoxing.

Detoxification is good and should be encouraged throughout your healing because it is important to expose yourself to things that will assist your purge while you are vulnerable. This chapter will focus on detoxifying and rebuilding your focus in order to propel you to your new beginning and foster positive change. We will first create a focus to live by, and then reorganize our desires, because everything we do is first created from the thoughts in our mind. Through discipline, we will begin to understand the importance of consciously and repeatedly addressing that focus. I'll also invite you to learn what could happen if you fail to mentally detox your focus, by explaining what happened to me when I failed to adhere to the detox process prior to moving on to another relationship. If you do not address this matter, your contaminated desires can lead you astray. Remember, you have to actually put into action and live by these recommendations in order to fully reap the benefits. By detoxifying your focus, you are reconfiguring your way of thinking and living.

Now that we have established the importance of building a foundation to live on, we are officially ready to start building interests of our own, in order to begin our life of healing, new memories, and a new focus. While focusing your energy on change, be very careful as to what emotions you entertain. Most importantly, get familiar with why they want to be entertained. Is it because you are still too weak to say **no**, or because you have not tamed yourself into discipline yet? When your desires feel as though they are too difficult to control, it is normal for you to feel like running back to your ex, or finding an alternative love interest to ease the pain or loneliness. That is no different from a relapse or moving on to another substance for comfort. That is the wrong desire to indulge because all you are doing then is scratching an emotional itch, which is truly a fresh wound in need of healing. Your judgment is way off right now, so it would be a little difficult to scout for true potential. I'm not saying it can not happen, I'm just saying, given your current state, it would be very challenging to maintain a healthy relationship. Just remember from Chapter 1, don't sabotage your future with your baggage. Take yourself back to the time *before* you were introduced to your addiction. Look at your situation from a perspective of someone who is not addicted, instead of that of one who is addicted. When you act how you want to be, you become what you act. Practice at being your best because *you can not give your absolute best if you are not your best*. When you train your focus for success, you engineer the structure of your discipline.

New Territory

Mentally venture off into unfamiliar territory. This unfamiliar territory I'm referring to is **you**, in your current state and as an individual. You are not the same person you were 10 years ago. You are not the same person you were five years ago, and you are definitely not the same person you were before you became addicted. Each experience in your life molds your character some way, form, or fashion. While in a relationship, it is natural to share your attention with your partner, because you are growing with the person. Your focus is growing with that person, and that person is always kept in mind when you do things. If not, then the repercussion of not thinking about the person probably burdens you. Now that life has changed, you have to figure a way to adapt to your new life. Maybe you are used to being held in bed, or maybe you are used to checking in before you leave or come home. Perhaps you are not used to holding yourself accountable for your actions. Whatever it is, I'm pretty sure that your routine has changed if you have decided to make a change. You need to get your mind off of your old routine and on to the voyage to familiarizing yourself to your new territory, so that you can refocus on what needs to happen moving forward.

Addicts think, sleep, breathe, and live their addiction. When a drug addict goes to rehab, it is in an effort to remove himself from what he cannot resist. It also works as a way to detoxify his thoughts, will, and focus. However long you have been attached to your addiction is how long you have been detached from your individuality. This is also the case if you have simply moved from one addiction/relationship to the next, as an escape from the pain. If you have never given yourself a chance to heal properly and learn the new you after each addictive experience, then you are simply bringing one problem to the next, and you are only escaping your freedom. If you can not honestly feel content alone, then your past and current hurts suppressed your emotional freedom. Detoxifying your focus first will acknowledge, and then release all of those past hurts and denials. You will be able to live with yourself without depending on anything else for happiness.

Breaking away from an addiction is very difficult, because we may not know how, or when, to detach before moving on. When we attempt to move on while still holding on to the addiction, we find ourselves moving on with life, but still attached to the burden of discomfort, which only slows us down because we are not living life to our fullest potential. I even have heard of some cases where individuals become so attached to an addiction that when they stop cold turkey, they are not able to survive. Perhaps the reason for this is because the mind convinced the body that it was completely dependent on the addiction. In essence, complete control was lost and surrendered to the addiction. If you are reading this book, then I believe you have not ventured that far off into demise, because your search for freedom exudes an inkling of hope. If you have even an inkling of hope, then you have not lost complete control. If you are searching for a solution or exit strategy, then that should tell you that you have enough control to make the decision to change. If you do not allow yourself to get it all out, then you could find yourself on a disastrous rollercoaster again. Detoxifying your focus means that you are cleansing your mind and life as you knew it from this addiction. There are several ways to detoxify your focus, but first let me explain to you what happened when I neglected to detoxify my focus and gave in to my desires prematurely.

Emotional Rollercoaster Ride— From one Problem to the Next

I made several very good attempts to rid myself of my second ex, but my desire for instant satisfaction eventually overpowered my determination. I tried taking a shortcut to healing but ended up relapsing by running away and into another situation. I made a drastic move in my life while trying to force myself to leave my second ex. It was clear that I did not have enough willpower to do it alone, and I hated the emotional state I was in. After almost four years, he still could not get it together, so I decided to take a job overseas and moved to the Middle East. Little did I know I only was prolonging emotional dissatisfaction. Had I detoxified my focus, I would not have been so gullible and anxious to find a replacement. I would have been more focused on building my strength and character back up. In order to work in the Middle East, I had to go through three weeks of training and medical screening to prepare for the austere conditions. During the three-week preparation process, I met someone new.

The New Guy, Ex #3

When I saw him, I immediately hoped he would be my prince charming. He took me out on our first date to Bennigan's restaurant and a movie. He opened my door and was very respectful. He really made me feel special, too. After our first few conversations, I thought we had a lot in common, zodiac signs and all. I figured he was God fearing, because he was practicing his faith and attended church regularly. No need to screen this one! I told him all about my previous relationship experiences and how I was treated (bad idea, but we will get into that in Chapter 8), and of course he listened and assured me that he would never do such a thing. This new guy really seemed to be into me, and so I suddenly abandoned my progress and the issues that needed tending. I had been starving for this type of attention for years. The new guy was different from my other exes because we shared some of the same family values and religion. I thought our union was perfect because he was also traveling to the Middle East, and had all the attributes my broken heart thought it needed. He was very polite and affectionate, held my hand in public when we would go out, blessed me after each sneeze, and even prayed over each of our meals. It was almost as if he was trained for marriage because he even washed, ironed, and hung my laundry while I was at work, to save me time, so we could spend more of it together. It felt too good to be true. Having not gotten over my second ex, I pursued this guy with all I had left. I was so happy to have someone who seemed to have great potential that I ran full speed and head first with this guy. I talked at a hundred miles an hour so that I could get everything he needed to know about me out and he was quiet. I thought he was a great listener, but he did not need to say anything, I was doing all the legwork for him. He did not need to work for me because he knew he already had me. It was a wrap!

    I was so eager to move on that I failed to recognize the telltale signs. I never actually got to know the guy until it was too late. I had fallen into a trap I helped make. I wanted to share love that was built on commitment and loyalty, have someone to go home to at night, and maybe someday get married, too. I brought this same focus to the relationship with the new guy without first screening to see if he was worthy of that kind partnership. I never took the time to really get to know him before falling for him. I did not guard my heart, affection, or emotions. I fell in love with the thought of being in love, and he happened to be the recipient. I was excited to be able to say that I was happy again, even though it was blind and superficial. I never healed from the hurt of my past. I was still bitter, and little did I know that I was only attracting what I was at the time. It all seemed so great at the beginning. He made me feel as though he was just as in love with me, if not more. His story was that he had never been in a real relationship before, and I was his first girlfriend, and his first love. That gave me security and made me feel as though I had come across a rare man, or better yet, I was significant to him for being the first woman to capture his heart. Every time he would tell me he loved me, it fueled my empty heart; even though I knew deep down inside that I was moving way too fast and too soon. I tried hiding our progress from family and friends because I knew they would shake their heads at how fast we were moving. They would certainly tell me about me, and I did not want to hear all that. It was enough that I was not listening to my own conscience telling me to slow down and pay attention to the telltale signs. I tried telling myself that it was okay, and justified my behavior by ignoring potential flaws because I felt I deserved to enjoy companionship. I even ignored warnings from others who knew him in our training class, writing it off as, "They just don't want to see me happy." It is crazy how we easily justify and follow

Detoxifying Your Focus

what we know in our heart is wrong, but yet have a hard time following what we know is right.

We already were talking about marriage one month into the relationship. I thought I had escaped the detoxifying stage of healing because I was ready to marry this guy and fight off any lingering baggage after the excitement of our rendezvous got old. I was so intoxicated in infatuation that no one could tell me anything because I was not willing to listen. Evidently, the new guy had some cleaning up to do himself. A few months into our relationship, while in Afghanistan, his cell phone rang, and I answered it.

"Hello?" I said.

On the other end was a woman responding in an unfamiliar, native tongue saying, "ello!" "my husband!" "ello!"

At first I thought to myself, this must be a local Afghan dialing the wrong number, so I hung up. Well, this woman called again, and again, but because she was speaking broken English, all I could understand was "Who is this?" "I want my husband!" This time, the sound "husband" was as profound as someone hitting me in the face with a sack of bricks. She spoke so intensely that I was a little convinced that this woman did not have the wrong number. Though the connection was really bad, I grew so annoyed, and I thought to myself, in disbelief and regret, "I know I am not dating a married man." I eagerly wanted to get to the bottom of this, but it was difficult, because she did not seem to understand anything I was saying. I spoke very slowly and asked, by his name, if he was her husband. She only replied with, "I want my husband."

I tried rephrasing the question several different ways, but she only became angry and hung up in my face, never clarifying if he was her husband. That uncertainty was my little hope of certainty that my prince charming was not too good to be true.

I wanted so badly to question him about this phone call when he returned from work, but I was unsure how to present this type of information to him. We had not had problems like this in the relationship; everything was always great. If it was a prank call (which I so hoped it was), I did not want him to think I did not trust him. I walked up and down the pavement, trying to figure a strategy on how I was going to present my suspicion to him. I did not know him well enough to know when or if he lied or told the truth. I felt as though I needed to be smart about my inquiry because all I knew was that I needed to know the truth. I decided to give him the benefit of doubt and simply approach him with complete honesty by telling him exactly what had happened. After explaining what happened, you would think it deserved a response, but he was quiet. My heart grew cold and desperate at his lack of expression. I, at least, expected certainty that he was not married, or even a shock that someone would call his phone with this type of accusation. I got *nada*! At this point, I just wanted to know if he was married, so I asked, "Are you married?"

He responded by looking at me in a way as if to say, "You know you are my first love; of course, I'm not married," but the words never came out his mouth. In fact, his next move was questioning me about the phone call in detail. He wanted to know exactly what was said. Knowing that I already had provided him with this information, and him having failed to answer my only question, I was convinced he was lying to me. This became our first official argument. While arguing, I studied him and everything he said, even his expression when he delivered his messages. The thought of this call being real was winning in my conscience. After he realized that I was not answering any more of his questions until he answered mine, he then asked, "Why did you even pick up my phone, or better yet, ask questions?" I was flabbergasted at his ridiculous outburst; we had never before had an issue with answering each other's phones and our relationship was open, or at least that is what I thought. Fed up, I asked him one more time and explained that if he did not answer my question, I was out. Finally, he answered my question with one word, "no," in an unconvincing tone. I was getting nowhere with him, so I decided to let it go, and left the conversation alone, for the moment. While I tried to play catch up with learning the ins and outs of this guy, I studied his character and personality by recollecting our whole argument.

My next few days were consumed with how I was going to figure out a way to get the truth, or at least satisfaction for my conscience. The phone never rang again, and I had nothing but his unconvincing words to stand on. I decided to regroup and figure out a strategy that would address my suspicions. I vacillated over calling his mother, because I had never spoken to her before, but I was desperate to get to the bottom of it. I did not know what type of person she was, or what to expect, but I was willing to walk the trial-by-error road for the truth. He spoke highly of his mother and claimed he told her about me. In fact, he assured me that his whole family back at home knew of me and was eager to meet me. At this point, I was not sure if any of that was true, but I used it as my push to call anyway. I told myself, if he was lying about his mother knowing me, then he was lying about being married. Trying to stay optimistic, I thought certainly she should know about me, or at least know about my existence in her son's life.

I called his mother and politely introduced myself; then asked her if she knew of me. She explained that she had heard of me, but in the capacity of a friend in her son's life. Of course, I was not alarmed at that because people introduce and refer to their love interests as friends all the time. I further explained that we were more than friends and were planning to take our relationship to the next level. I then explained my suspicion, the phone call, and then cut straight to the chase and flat out said, "I'd like to ask you a few questions about your son before we move on to the next level of our relationship." Surprisingly, she was all ears and willing to answer any question I had about her son. I began to ask the big question! "Is your son marri...?"

Before I could finish, she cut me off and freely gave me the truth. She said, "Yes, my son is married." It was almost as if she was giving me a get-out-of-jail-free card, or it was routine for women to call and confirm the status of her son. Either way, her words immediately snatched any other questions I'd plan to ask straight from my thoughts. I was speechless. Immediately my chest turned cold inside as the shock of desperation filled my emotions. At that moment, my confusion ceased and my heart turned heavy. Devastating news always seemed to have that type of effect on me. She began to explain certain particulars about the marriage, but I was not processing anything she said. All I could think was, I knew better then to move so fast, and my family and friends tried to warn me.

The new guy was a church-going man, but had a habitual lying problem, and unfortunately was emotionally unconscious. His mother confirmed that his wife, who was of Hispanic decent, lived in Italy and spoke very little English. The new guy was bilingual, and only spoke to his wife in Spanish. That explained why she was not responding when I tried to find out what really was going on. Running away from my problems without detoxifying my focus only had led to bigger problems. I had fallen for a married man. I now had international love problems to add to the pain I was trying to avoid by replacement. Even though many may believe a few months was still fresh enough to get out, you would be surprised how fast your disastrous addiction will seek to find the next best fix when you lack discipline and disregard truth. The fact of the matter is that when you jump headfirst into a situation without healing yourself; you basically are surrendering the little control you had left. Once you do this, you give yourself very little chance to unravel from disappointment. Deeper into the addiction you go.

His rebuttal to this news was that he mistakenly had married this girl, while stationed in Italy; a legal paper mix-up when they applied for her to visit the United States as his spouse. He further explained that he did not consider them married because they never had a religious ceremony. I could not accept the excuse of accidental marriage. The worst part was that I knew I was tangled now, because I was standing there expecting some type of explanation after his mom had confirmed my suspicion. Even though I was in disbelief of his explanation, I wanted it to be true. Therefore, I chose to make it the truth in order to avoid the pain of another breakup. He assured me that he was no longer with the "soon to be ex-wife," and that he did, in fact, love me and still wanted us to be together. Had I not been so busy trying to find a replacement, I would have been able to guard myself from this disaster. Emotionally addicted again, I ended up trying to make it work under the assumption that he was getting divorced. I was worse off than when I was with my second ex, and even more terrified to be alone, especially being so far away from home. I had not understood the importance of detoxifying my focus until I found myself making the same mistakes again. My mother used to chant to me, "If you always do what you always did, you will always get what you always got." Those words rang the truth so clearly to me. However, as you can see, the new guy and I had more in common then we both actually realized. Do you see what I had attracted? We both were running from previous relationships, and I just happened to be the unmarried one. I truly believe you attract what you are. He was looking for a replacement, emotionally damaged, trying to run away from it all, and so was I.

After getting to know the new guy, I learned that he did not understand the extent of effort needed to make a serious relation-

Detoxifying Your Focus

ship work, but I was willing to work through that. He was mentally immature, and we were morally incompatible, and still, I wanted to work through that. Lastly, imagine this: We found out that we did not even like each other after getting to know each other, but if he was willing, I was so addicted that I was willing to learn how to like him. Though we shared the same religion, we had different beliefs, thus making the two of us unequally yoked. It would have never worked anyway, but do you think I was trying to hear that? At this point, I was willing to work through anything to feed my addiction of needing a companion. I simply skipped all the details and rushed straight into **love** without truly getting to know this guy. I allowed myself to become so possessed by his charm that I completely neglected to look past his outer attributes, charm, religion, and zodiac sign.

Once you are strong enough to completely detoxify your focus, you will be able to see clearly what you needed in a mate, not what you can tolerate just to have a mate. It is not fair to your well-being to maintain a relationship with a partner out of default because you are not strong enough to wait for the right one. Do yourself a favor, detoxify your focus, because then you will be able to determine who belongs in your radar as a prospective candidate to your heart. You will acquire the skills to do this, because through detoxifying your focus, you change the way you see yourself, your future, and your goals. This transformation will force you into becoming aware of what you require to be happy. Don't settle for getting what you can get out of pity. This is your life, for crying out loud! Picking a partner is one of the most important decisions in life, if not *the* most important personal decision. Whatever you do, just be sure that when you pick your partner, it is when you are at an emotionally healthy stage in life.

Polygraph Test

Years into the relationship, I continued to notice an increased pattern of deceit from ex number three. It seemed that we argued more about whether or not he was lying about something than we did over anything else. He believed in his own lies and based his arguments on those lies and wanted me to build our foundation from that. I could not find contentment with that. Years into our relationship, we still had not broken ground for growth. We were still working on trust, and therefore, could not build anything until we had at least established that. The relationship raveled in empty promises. He lied so habitually that I gave him an ultimatum to either take a lie detector (polygraph) test to prove his loyalty, or we would have to split, and he agreed to take the test. I researched polygraph administers and found a licensed guy in my area who was highly recommended by legal services. Limited to only four questions during the polygraph, I asked about the suspicion I had of him cheating with two specific ex-lovers, random prostitutes, and, lastly, the ex-wife. I wanted to know if he had been with the ex-wife sexually since we had been together as a couple. Sadly enough, he failed every single question. Even after he failed every question, I *still* wanted him to get right for me. I remembered pouring my heart out and explaining how I wanted to be treated, and what he should say and feel if he wanted to get me back. Truth be told, I was not fed up yet and still wanted to cling on instead of move on. He was the type of person that never apologized for his wrongdoings unless someone reminded him. So, I catered to his inadequacies by reminding him to apologize to me in order to compensate for his shortcomings. Before I continue on, let me just tell you now, when a person genuinely loves you, you do not have to tell him how to love you, or what to do to show you he loves you. You certainly should not have to coach him on how to apologize or feel remorse when he has clearly hurt you. When a person truly loves you, he only will deal with you through the heart. His heart will make him say and do the things that a person who genuinely loves you will say and do. Trust me when I say that there is no mistaking when someone genuinely loves you for you, and not for what you have or the feeling you ignite within him when you are around. You want someone to love you for *you* and not for how you make them feel. That is what you call selfish loving because eventually, when the feeling that you ignite within him fades away, so will his so-called love.

Instead of an apology, ex number three reverted to silence or dangled marriage when he was caught in his lies. He was silent because he figured that, eventually, I would be the one to break the silence. If I did not break the silence, he dangled marriage in order to spark my interest again. It was almost as if that was his defense mechanism, or default setting when he'd mess up really badly. For him to bring up marriage, it made me think he felt for me the way I would feel for a person I wanted to marry. This type of feeling you just do not feel for anyone, and if you are really lucky, this feeling lasts long enough for a lifetime, and for just one person. Therefore, because he brought up marriage, I felt as though I should help him formulate the words that would allow him to win me over and get us back together.

I actually thought that if I formulated the words, he would be in agreement, nodding right along with me. I wanted to see remorse in him, and thought that giving him the answers to my puzzle would show him how he needed to feel in order to make amends. My focus was all wrong. I should not have been telling him how to win me over if he had no desire to seize the opportunity to do it himself. After expressing my views on how valuable I should be to him, his response was more than unsettling. The conversation, via instant messaging, went like this. I wrote to him:

> *"After all this time and everything we have been through, I would expect you to have more to say to me if you truly wanted marriage. I would at least expect you to say...*
>
> *I do not deserve you, but I can promise you that I will live the rest of my life as the man you do deserve, from here moving forward. I have hurt you more times then I care to admit, and I am deeply*

sorry for the pain I have caused you. I have made the biggest mistake of my life because you mean the world to me. I never want to lose you. Whatever I can do to make us right will be my new focus. We have to get back on track if I am still what you want. From here on out, I will be open to you in every way. No more secrets! No more lies! I will give you what you deserve. When I tell you I love you, I am telling you that my heart craves you, and to be next to you. I will do everything I possibly can to make you happy, because your happiness is the most important thing to me. I am grateful to God for sending you to me, and for such a beautiful gift, I owe it to God to take care of you. I owe it to God to love you and to be honest with you. Please, consider the possibility of us starting a fresh new beginning. I love you, and I only want you. Whatever I can do, I will do starting with you knowing that nothing else in this world matters more to me than you. You are everything to me. I am begging you to consider the possibility of us again, because I am sorry for what I've done. I LOVE YOU, La'Donna."

After writing what I expected him to say and feel, he replied with:

"This is why we will never be, because you need to get your ass off your high horse."

I could not believe his response. Sure, my expectations might have been considered a bit much if it was merely a casual relationship, but I thought we were more than that. In my mind, I felt lucky to have him, and viewed our relationship serious enough for marriage. He, on the other hand, had no remorse or respect, and was therefore, not the man deserving of my hand in marriage. He did not have the ability to see me in the way I saw him, or better yet, the way I saw myself. He was comatose to his wrongdoing. If he could not reconcile his faults with God, there was no way he ever could care enough to reconcile with me. I had so much love for him, but he could not care enough to reciprocate the love through his actions because he was stuck on worldly pleasures. All this time, I had thought our understanding of love, or lack thereof, was on two different pages, when actually we were in two totally different books. I knew what I had to do, but I really did not want to go through the inevitable pain. In some strange way, I knew he cared for me, but on his own level of compassion, and that level was simply not sufficient enough to sustain me or make me happy. I dared not mope around about why my value was nothing to him. It's just like holding a two-dollar toy car and a $100 dollar bill in front of a boy, then asking him to make a choice as to which one he wants. The kid would most likely choose the toy, because he does not have a mature mind to understand that $100 dollars is more valuable and could buy him plenty more toy cars. In his mind, all he sees is value in the toy car, because it gives him what he wants,–immediate pleasure. Like many people, the kid's mind does not understand value, so he chooses what is valuable to him. That doesn't make it wrong; it just means that sometimes what some may deem valuable may not be to others. That is why it is so important to truly know your partner so that you can understand what is valuable to that person before you invest your heart.

GETTING IT ALL OUT OF YOUR SYSTEM

I remember getting so angry one moment, and then, in the next moment, I just wanted ex number three near to console my grief. It was crazy. I was on an emotional rollercoaster. The fact of the matter was that I was simply juggling a load of hidden emotional disappointments. I had to get it all out; there was no getting around it. I knew that I was not strong enough to stop cold turkey, but I was hopeful that, in time, I could wean myself off slowly but surely. I tried to prepare myself for the gradual transition, by reminding myself of the goal every time I was tempted to go back. I knew the final step was to deny my thoughts of the possibility of our getting back together in order to get it out of my system. However, in order to reach this point, I first had to see myself as an individual unattached to my circumstance. What I wanted was to be happy as an individual and rid myself from all of my past hurts. At this point, I was polluted with disappointments, and there was no way I could truly detoxify if, as soon as one left, I immediately was looking for a replacement. I could not have a backup man on speed dial, either. I was too emotionally fragile to find a healthy partner. I could not go on a manhunt looking for a man to shower me with sympathy on my deficiency. From the look of things, I would become the prey, and the man would end up hunting me. My focus needed to be on purifying myself. I simply had to prepare to let go of everything, but I was not sure if I was ready for that just yet.

Reluctantly, I decided to move forward by using a goal instead of a partner to build my future. Instead of trying to find my next "good-enough" partner, I chose to pour positive attributes into my own cup. I went back to school, this time with a focus to finish with honors, not to pass the time away. I was slowly ridding myself of toxins by adding other positive responsibilities to my life. Focusing on me and facing my demons assisted in severing the pain from my system. You have to plant in your mind that the only option to success is focusing on the new goals you place in your mind. Everything else is simply details to throw you off. Finding a replacement will not complete the job. Convincing yourself you can not take these steps will not do the job, either. You have to build internal strength and use every force of energy within your body, as if you were breaking out of chains, and roar yourself into the decision to focus on you. Let go of all those demons.

If you have gone around in circles, you must end that cycle and focus your thoughts, the same way you focus on a certain subject you would like to master, or that addiction you have to feed. Your old focus could have been your everyday struggles as to how you can not get over your addiction because you can not fathom life without it. What you must do is take that energy and

Detoxifying Your Focus

put it toward what life would have been, had you not ever been introduced to the addiction. I actually role-played this thought in my mind. I thought back to the time before I was afflicted with emotional disappointments. I thought back to the days when I was Babygirl and my family was a complete unit. Those days, I dreamed of unthinkable possibilities for my life. That was a time I felt unconditional love. When you think back to the time before you were emotionally inflicted, feel the joy and rid yourself from negativity. When you filter yourself, squeeze out all of the things that you do not like about yourself, and what you did not favor about yourself while under the addiction's spell. Push out whatever is not healthy for you. Yes, this is probably going to hurt when you realize the truth, but you must understand that this suffering will be used to build character. When you are set apart, you become more holy and focused. Sometimes, we can get so consumed by the world that our senses become numb to distractions and demise. Don't allow yourself to become oblivious to demise, because it will throw you back into old habits faster than you even can realize you have taken 10 steps backwards. Every move you make and every thought you think, make it all about you. Put your own well-being first for a change and abandon your addiction. Think of yourself as finally being released from an emotional prison. Now is your opportunity to make a better life for yourself. Don't derail. Keep your eyes and focus on the prize, which is securing independence.

You may recognize that there are some deficiencies related to old disappointments. Uncover, target, and then get rid of all those unhealthy disappointments and desires. Cater to your deficiencies by treating them with balanced care instead of suppressing yourself. When I first started the process of healing, I had many demons to deal with. Those demons were confusion, regret, disappointment, psychological relapses, bitter/sweet anger, irrational mood swings, and withdrawals, just to name a few. Keep in mind, all of these feelings are normal when you are detoxing from addictive emotional attachments. The good news is, if you don't give in, they will go away, provided you remain firm and strong.

Scream and cry if you have to, to get it out. However, just remember to try not to think about the addiction. You have to train your thoughts to diffuse this occurrence. Anytime your mind tries to sneak in the addiction, immediately stop it! This means you have to always be conscious of what you think. Rebuke the thoughts as soon as you notice them, and do not ever get caught idle-minded. Are you tired yet? I told you it was not going to be easy. Just remember, anything worth having is worth working hard for; after all, you will appreciate and hold it dearer to you that way. Get in shape mentally and emotionally, and detoxify your focus. If you allow yourself a second to indulge in the thought of that addiction, you are tempting yourself, and you will eventually give in. It's like a muscle memory of the brain; you will eventually overcome the control of your thoughts, and the cravings will diminish over time. Remain patient and keep steady. Remind yourself constantly that you have complete control over your thoughts.

Detoxifying Your Focus

WHERE TO GO FROM HERE

Chances are you wish you could have a different circumstance now that you are beginning the early stages of healing. I was there once. I wanted to know why I could not be happy with a companion, or why things were not going so well for me. I was only focusing on the negative though. Things always can be worse. I've learned that keeping a positive mind and attitude work mysteriously well in maintaining a happy life. Do you ever wonder why people sometimes want what they don't have, then they become miserable because they focus on not having what they want? Try loving what you do have and your current life because that is one of the best ways to position yourself to receive, through positive thinking.

I worked with a lady who always complained about others having what she did not. She often times gossiped about the accomplishments of others, and would question, in an envious tone whether or not they deserved it. For instance, she would come to work spreading the news of how someone else got a promotion, and would then say that they did not deserve it. She complained about how someone else just bought a new home, and would then say, but they can not afford it. It seemed as if she was unhappy within her own world because she could not be genuinely happy for anyone else. It was as if someone else's gain forced her to face her own failure. She always complained about what she did not have and what others did have, but was not doing anything to obtain the things she saw others receiving. She thought complaining and obsessing over it would change her circumstance, but she was obsessed with negativity. To be honest, her life was just fine in my eyes. She just did not see it. She was a single, middle-aged woman making a six-figure salary and had no major responsibilities like kids, or a house. She was way too preoccupied with following the events of other people's lives that she had little time to focus on herself. I shared my observation with her and thought that maybe if she optimized her own talents, she would change the way she saw everyone else's growth. She would never progress if she continued to focus on the lives of others and not her own. After our talk, she applied what she felt could work for her life. She stopped complaining and gossiping about other co-workers and focused more on what she wanted. She still talked about everyone, but this time without the negative stuff. She now resides in the home she has always wanted and decided to open her own business, working out of her home, in a capacity that makes her happy.

Have you ever heard someone talk badly about a close relative, but he dares not allow someone else to do the same thing, justifying it because that's his loved one and, right or wrong, he would stand by them? Perhaps you have heard them say, "That's my relative and I wouldn't trade him/her in for anything in this world, good or bad." That's how you have to look at your own life experiences and situations. Make the best of it, and dare not to trade it in for anything in the world. In order to be a positive person at all times, you have to learn how to love the good and the bad. We can sit here and complain about what we wish we had or where we wish we could be. The fact of the matter is that you have to learn

Detoxifying Your Focus

to love yourself and your circumstances no matter what. That is where you go from here.

Have you ever heard people remark that some of the happiest people in this world are poor? It's because they learned to be 100 percent happy within. My brother, Gabriel, used to drive a beaten up 1991 convertible Pontiac Sunbird; he loved that car. One day he was driving down the 110 highway and his convertible top got caught in the 65-mile-an-hour wind. It demolished his top. He was so hurt but he never thought about abandoning his car. Even if a brand new Mercedes Benz drove up, he certainly did not feel intimidated or that he had underachieved. He was completely content with his level of living because he knew where he was going and was confident in his growth. I know some well-off people, similar to my co-worker, who made six-figures and had minimal responsibilities, and yet they still wish they were someone else. It starts with you appreciating yourself. You have to think of yourself as an individual and focus on optimizing that person, so that you can find confidence in your growth and be your very best.

So, you are hurting and can not stand the fact that you do not have what you want at the moment. Well, learn to love your experience because it's your experience, and you should never want to trade it in for anything. You will learn from this stage in life. Right now, find something that will ignite immediate excitement. It needs to be healthy though. Do something you have not done in a long time, like roller-skating or whatever made you happy as a kid. Go back to those days for a moment, or any time that made you feel worry-free and alive. Invite your new focus to explore things that will give you new, positive memories. Whatever you do, don't go to substances to numb your feelings. Add that to your list of things that are **not options** for your healing. The last thing you want to do is numb your feelings. Go through the pain! Pain is normal when you are healing. Trust me, you will appreciate yourself more for having been so strong. I did, and it built my character and confidence. There were some nights when the pain was so strong that I hardly could stand it. Because giving into the pain was not an option, by default, all I could do was drop to the floor and cry my heart out. I was like a late-night wolf crying my heart out in the dark, moaning in emotional agony. The pain of withdrawal was so intense that I think I cried until I had no more tears to shed. My eyes wept until they turned red, and I was so physically weak that I did not care about the struggle anymore. I had no desire or strength to feed the addiction, nor did I have a feeling of abandonment. I was basically neutral and felt freed from everything. It was a piece of serenity, and I was content because I knew that I was, again, suffering for the better good. It is wise to suffer doing good than to suffer for destruction. I found comfort in knowing that I was doing the right thing, and the only other way to go from there was in the right direction because I had hit rock bottom, and had starved those intense desires to find a replacement for my heart. With this new beginning, I knew it was time to start nurturing myself so that I would grow properly. I took charge by staying focused and crying it out. By facing the pain, I was able to direct one-on-one healing over the force that was trying to break me inside. I got familiar with the hurt, instead of running away, and by doing that, I did not let the pain control me. Instead, I controlled the pain and even found serenity at the end of the battle. After that painful episode, I really felt as though I had conquered defeat to reach a huge milestone. I knew I still had a ways to go, but I made it through that storm. Every time you go through your strongest pain, it is you leaving one stage of life and transitioning to your new life. Keep in mind, each storm you make it through will allow you to grow stronger and give you the experience and know-how to make it through your next rough episode.

Be Mindful of Distractions

There will be so many external, and internal, distractions trying to keep you from attaining your goal. To remain focused, it is imperative that you control what you expose yourself to during this detoxification stage, and this includes the people you choose to expose yourself to, and the conversations you have with them. Taking control means you will have to filter your exposure.

Environment

Aside from the pull of discomfort, I'm sure before you decided to detoxify your focus that your routine seemed to be pretty normal. Now that you are making a conscious effort to change and detoxify yourself, any memory of the past could shock you back into depression. In order to prepare for those mishaps, change everything around you. Rearrange your place of living, or where you spend most of your time. Reorganize your closet, change your bedding and linens, change the scent of your environment with a new fragrance, and even rearrange your medicine cabinet if you have to in order to detox your focus. When you change your everyday routine, it all allows you to form new memories with yourself outside of what you are used to. Different scents and fragrances have a way of igniting new and old memories, and can be used as a way to start the reconfiguration of your new focus, on your terms. You are subconsciously taking yourself out of a familiar comfort zone and exposing yourself to something new.

After my breakup, and during my detox stage, I failed to change my surrounding environment. Why didn't I heed my own advice? I guess I thought, for a moment, that I was strong enough not to have to completely rearrange my environment. Well, again, I was wrong. Without expecting it, I woke up one morning and went to the same spot I had been going to out of routine, the bathroom, but this time my heart dropped when I saw ex number three's hygiene items laying just the way he left them. I hadn't even touched them; I had never touched them. It really crushed me because I now was fighting a reason to contact him. That fast, I resorted to justifying how I could contact him. I know this may seem small and insignificant, but when your addiction to something is in need of some attention, even the smallest things matter in your detox stage. Once I arrived at the stage in which I needed to detox my focus, my cravings were fighting for me to fail. Please, for your own good, change your environment, because it will provoke change within you. You can even take it one step further and change your voicemail greeting, like in the movie "Two Can Play That Game," or the route you normally take to get to work, since that is also an everyday occurrence. Reorganize the pictures on your home or office wall and your furniture. Sit in a different seat at work or in class, just make it different for you. When you detox your outer surrounding, you, in essence, detox your inward environment because your mind is forced to think differently. That is how you form new memories for yourself.

Communication

If you attract the people you used to be like, and the people you are used to hanging around, you will fall back into the trap of addictions. You need to change everything; it is for your own good. Dismiss the friends who do not have your best interests at heart, and distance yourself from the friends who will not help your progress. The main goal is to change your heart. It will take time, but every decision you make must be with your heart in mind. Eventually, after you feed your heart with positive things, it will begin to exude great things. Everything you do, without realizing it, will be expressed through your heart.

When you communicate with people, stay mindful of where the conversation is taking you and how the conversation makes you feel. When you detox your focus, you have to guard everything to which you expose yourself. Some people may not even be aware that whatever they're communicating to you may be hindering your progress. For instance, at this stage, you do not want to have conversations with anyone that will discourage your improvement, or negatively impact your aura. Right now, you have to surround yourself with positive things. Be careful as to the people you listen to, and the advice you heed, because you may be being led by the wrong energy. Keep your eyes on the prize and, remember, detoxifying your focus is all about building your endurance of discipline. As mentioned earlier, you do not want to expose yourself to someone who does not truly have your best interests at heart. You will know whether or not this person has your best interests at heart by the way the conversation makes you feel at the end of the day. Think about the conversations you have, and think about their root. This is only for you to decipher. No one else can do this for you, because deep down inside, only you truly know what is best for you, based on your goals. Utilize your skills of wisdom, and if you do not feel that you have it, then simply ask yourself for it, and it will come. Close your eyes, visualize your wisdom, and now tell yourself, "I want to be exposed to wisdom," and believe it! With wisdom, you will understand that words are very powerful! With that said, understand that when you communicate, you must also be mindful to where *you* take the conversation as well. Just don't dwell on anything negative. When you communicate, speak positively about everything, this will help you through detoxifying your focus.

Music

Music has a way of changing a person's mood in a split second. Music can make you feel invincible, fly, and sexy, like you want to go out and party, or it can make you feel like you are in love or wish you were. In my case, some songs make me feel like I can dance, and Lord knows I can not freestyle dance! Music can pump you up enough to get in a good workout, but then again, music can have the exact reverse effect. Sometimes it can make you feel sad, guilty, or just plain bad. Music can reawaken your memory to anything, depending on how it affected you in the past. With that being said, music can also form new memories. If you want to vividly remember something, all you have to do is play a song over and over again; it then will act as a soundtrack to that part of your life. What you feed yourself has a direct reflection of what you put out and how you act; that is why guarding yourself is very important. When you guard the music you listen to, you are guarding your mood swings and how you feel. Music can change our moods unconsciously, without us even realizing it. For this reason alone, it is very important that while you are detoxifying your focus, you monitor what music you listen to, so you do not fall into emotional depression from old feelings. You do not want to trap your fragile state of being in old memories through familiarity with the past or because a song reminds you of the old times. Even if the music does not ignite old feelings, be mindful of the feelings it does awaken while you are in this healing process. You may be listening to music that makes you feel doubt and sorrow. If the music happens to direct your mood in that direction, change it. Do not listen to it until you have detoxified your focus and are strong enough not to allow it to alter or slow down your path to success. You need to stay encouraged, uplifted, and joyfully sparked with positive influences. My suggestion would be to rearrange your MP3 player and music collection so that when you listen to your music, your new music play list will provide you with positive, energetic feelings.

You need to know what works for you. When I'm going through hard times, gospel, classical, some jazz and soothing meditation music works for me, depending on what time of day it is or what mood I'm in. I love hip/hop, rap, R&B, and pop music as well, but I had to be cautious of the message that spilled into my space and the energy it provided. I listened to an Internet radio station called Pandora Radio, (www.pandora.com), in which I was able to make a radio station based on my mood. Get to know your music and find out what works for you. Don't be afraid to tap into a different genre of music, either. You may just find a new interest by exposing yourself to different things.

Pandora's Box

At this point in your healing process, you need to have a box labeled "Pandora's Box." It is a place for all the old pictures and music that you deem unhealthy at the moment or anything that will hinder your progress. If your pictures and music are all electronic, then label a folder "Pandora's Files," and move all of those files to that folder.

Detoxifying Your Focus

Don't look at it or open Pandora's Box/Files until you have finished this stage of healing and strong enough to handle what is in it.

Don't Skip a Beat

While learning to love your life through the good times and bad, add a little spice to the healing journey. Don't skip a beat just because you are alone. You should act the same way you would if you were in a relationship or trying to impress someone. Instead of sending flowers, candy, concert tickets, love letters, and gifts to your mate, send that stuff to yourself! This was the best part of my healing process, but there is a method to this process. The only way this will be exciting is if you do not expect it. This is what you do, and remember we are still detoxifying our focus. The focus is **you.**

Thank goodness for online shopping! Go online and get something small but sweet. This gift has to be something that, if your mate were to surprise you with it, melts your heart. Remember, nothing expensive; otherwise, you will be anticipating its arrival. It must be something you will forget about after you purchase it, but appreciate once you get it. Now, once you find that **inexpensive** gift, mail it to yourself and date the delivery two weeks later. In the meantime, write yourself a love letter and pour all of your emotions into this letter; leave nothing out. Tell yourself how beautiful and how strong you are. Remind yourself that you can not live without **you!** You can open as much of yourself as you would like to in this letter. No need to worry about exposing your deepest feelings because you can trust that the recipient of this letter will value those words like no other. Buy yourself a card! Act as if you were expressing the same feelings that you would expect someone else to have for you, if he genuinely loved you. Be sure to add words of encouragement and write "I Love You with all my heart," at the end of the letter. Try to change your own handwriting a little, so it will catch you off guard once you receive it. Next, either drop it in the mailbox, or if you decide to get an online card, make the delivery date several weeks into the future. Last, order yourself movie tickets and set a date and time to go. Don't be late, and don't allow anything or anyone to distract your focus from yourself. Many times we deny ourselves just to please others. I'm guilty of that! This is your time; it is imperative that you put you first. The purpose of this is to shower love and appreciation on *you*. It really works! Sooner, rather than later, you will have something to which to look forward.

<u>Holidays!</u> You need to shower so much joy on yourself that when the holiday arrives, you are so overjoyed with excitement that you can hardly contain yourself. I decorated for every holiday. Buycostumes.com was my favorite online decorating store. They had everything I needed. I went online and found all the holidays recognized in the USA, and I celebrated each one. I may not have gone all out for all of them, but I did recognize them all, until I felt good enough to move on to other excitements. Be sure to remain frugal, otherwise you will be cleaning up little confetti pieces every month, and that can become a little annoying after the third holiday. Remember, it is the thought that counts.

Detoxifying Your Focus

Valentine's Day! I did not mope around. I made my day special and relaxing. You are building your confidence again; utilize this time to get in touch with your heart and get to know who you are. Do whatever you need to do to make you remain special because there is only one *you*. So, give thanks for who you are! I ordered a cute little silk gown from Victoria's Secret. It was nothing provocative or anything that left me wishing that I had someone to see me in it. It was comfortable, but sexy enough to make me feel special. I was excited for Valentine's Day; I actually looked forward to it and planned my evening very well. It was a night of pampering and movie watching! I started out by lighting a few candles, as I enjoyed soft music, and then I relaxed in a tub of soothing bath oils. After my oil bath, I unwrapped the silk gown I ordered weeks before, and slid it on. I prepared a light meal for myself and decorated the eating area with rose pedals and more candles. I made sure to take pictures because this was a night to remember; it was beautiful and peaceful. After enjoying dinner and wine, I laid in my bed and finished my night with a movie. I was picking myself back up and enjoying every moment of it.

When you are without a companion, you should treat yourself the same way, if not better, as when you are with a companion. You have to set the bar for yourself if you expect to eventually get back into the dating scene, after you have healed. Try all of these things, instead of picking up on a bad habit. Whatever works for you, do it to keep that spark going in your life. Whatever you have to do to maintain focus and encourage happiness, do it.

You may be down on yourself, but don't skip a beat because you feel discouraged or you are fasting from your addiction. Understand that this is all just a moment in time. Look for the good in your situation. Your life is colorful right now because your emotions can encourage you to do the unthinkable. Now that you are focused, you can explore all of the cravings you have and why they affect you. That can be quite an event, because in exploring your cravings, you recognize character and poise. One day, you will share your journey with others. I love to sing, and singing makes me feel rejuvenated, so I made sure to find a karaoke spot and poured it all out. Keep in mind, these are all things that worked for me. It is up to you to find your niche, make it work, and run with it. Cater to your personality and character. If you know that you are an energetic, always-on-the-run type of person, then keep the excitement going by filling your schedule with new and exciting events. If you are the mellow type of person, continue the letters and even hide them somewhere in a textbook, closet, old coat pocket, drawer, pot, or any other unexpected place that will surprise you. Keep yourself excited by sending notes from the past you to the future you. You can do this by hiding letters now, which you will later find in the future. Perhaps, you can tell yourself what you would hope to be, and then see if you are that person once you find the letter. I would love to hear about some of the creative things you came up with to get you through your detoxification stage of healing. Keep your schedule busy, and by all means, don't skip a beat!

Detoxifying Your Focus

REFLECTION

If you become weak through your detoxifying stage, provide balance by reminding yourself of exactly what you want. Say to yourself constantly, exactly what you demand:

- I am in control.
- I am free from all addictions.
- I can live abundantly, while not depending on any substance or person.

Find a new excitement and focus your energy on that stimulation. Build new and positive memories for yourself, and don't get caught obsessing over the pain. The fact of the matter is, only you can optimize your worth.

When something is rare or limited, it becomes valuable because of its scarcity. Apply this same concept to yourself. Try to stay under the radar and silent until you are confident enough to get through the detoxifying stage. Become more valuable through scarcity. While you are missing in action, recovering, the absence of your presence will merit thoughts of inquiry into your well-being. Become scarce by filling your schedule to capacity. Once you have found inner strength, step out, and represent your new character. Keep in mind that you do not have to include everyone in your plans and/or the things you choose to do to get you through your healing. I would suggest that you not broadcast the changes you choose to make. Often, other people will not understand what you may have to do to get you where you need to be. Other times, some may attempt to discourage you from doing those necessary things, either advertently or inadvertently because your achievements and victory very well could be viewed as their failure. *Schadenfreude* is a German term best described as a pleasure derived from the misfortune of others. Sometimes, we act from *schadenfreude* in the way we think. Don't wish to become a victim of your circumstance. I have seen many people stay in their circumstances just to get sympathy from others, because somehow a pleasure is derived from the attention, but at their expense. Detox your focus, and do not talk or think yourself into the victim role because you become what you think and desire. Others around you may not even purposely, or openly, act from *schadenfreude*, because it is a secret enjoyment of someone's misfortune. Be cautious to the opinion of others because the advice could be coming from a person who secretly wants you to fail. Besides, it's not their walk; it's yours. I would suggest that you keep the intimate things you choose to do to yourself. By doing this, you are able to change your life, to your standards, without the opinion of discouragers.

It takes time to flush out the toxins from your past, but stay focused and keep flushing; you will get there. Keep your eyes on the prize, and remember what your goal is. As my brother always told me, "Goals, goals, goals are the key words." Goals are the tools to direct our actions. Without goals, we are shooting blind, hoping to hit our target. Yes, we might hit it by chance, but wouldn't it be more effective to open our eyes? Let's open our eyes and get a clear view of

Detoxifying Your Focus

our target. What is your ultimate goal? Where are you trying to get in the next five or ten years? Is it getting over your addiction, building positive relationships, emotional satisfaction or finding true happiness? Once you figure that out, you can forecast short-term/long-term goals based on that. Restricting our activities in a positive way is what *goals* do. The word *goal* is derived from the 1275-1325 Anglo-Saxon *gaelan,* which means to hinder or impede. The point is that it is imperative to question what needs to be restricted in our lives for the sake of what we need to reach our goals.

Once you have completely detoxified your focus, you will be able to effortlessly practice the suggestions explained in this chapter. When you practice discipline, it becomes your way of living. At the beginning, there will be a pull that wants you to stop detoxing your focus. This pull will seem to be stronger than your will, but you have to persevere. Through perseverance, the pull will weaken, and your will is going to strengthen. Eventually, your will is going to grow stronger than the pull, and then you will have control. Stay excited, because it will happen for you!

Moving along...
...to Chapter 4!

CHAPTER 4

Learning the New You & Finding Your True Value

THE HEALING CONTINUES

Two-thousand, nine hundred, and twenty-nine hours later, that's 122 days, or better yet, four whole months, I was clean, without my addiction. On day one, that kind of time seemed like a lifetime, and by day two, I could not even see that far into the future without my addiction. Strangely enough, I was still battling the hurt and loss of my addiction as if it was still day one. By this time, I had passed the mourning stages; instead, I now was hurting from simply being alone. Although I had made significant progress with my healing, I was beginning to forget all that I had gone through to get where I was at the time; I started to feel complacent. I knew my ex was slowly filtering out of my system, but I was far from happy. Four months into my progress, and still feeling pain, I was beginning to feel discouraged, because my healing was not moving fast enough. I needed something else to shock me back into encouragement, and fast. Therefore, I decided to take myself out, but this time, I took a trip down memory lane.

As you read the next section, imagine losing a significant amount of weight, say 100 lbs., and then forgetting the work you'd gone through to lose the weight. Now that you are comfortable, you begin to entertain the thought of old habits. However, just before you are tempted to go backwards, you find an old picture of yourself that suddenly shocks you back into your good senses because the picture reminds you of how far you have come.

ALL IN THE FRAGRANCE AND SOUNDTRACK

One cool, breezy night, I sat out by the lake for some personal time with myself, a date. I brought my iPod and earphones to keep me company. I sprayed Love Spell by Victoria's Secret all over my body. This was the fragrance I faithfully wore in the early stages of my healing. My soundtrack was Fred Hammond's album, Love Unstoppable. The fragrance and album had worked in concert to help get me through my time of distress, 122 days ago. I had listened to this album and worn that fragrance for six weeks straight before I got tired of it. I utilized the fragrance and music to remind me vividly of how far I'd traveled; sort of like the picture that shocks you back into your good senses. The fragrance distinctly reminded me of where I was and what I had gone through

Learning the New You & Finding Your True Value

to get this far. I had misrepresented my true progress, because 122 days ago I was picking myself up off the floor in agony, completely lost, not knowing how I was going to get through the next day. Now, I was calm enough to believe that there was light at the end of the tunnel. Though I still felt the hurt, I had gained so much more control over my actions and mind. It was just the moon, the stars, trees, a bench, and my reflection in the slightly ruffled water. It was peaceful and beautiful. I covered the bench with my blanket and laid on my back to gaze into the universe. Suddenly, it hit me: I realized that my last ex, number three, was not the only person filtering out of my system. There was additional residue from my second ex, and even my first love from my teenage years that needed cleaning.

I had never healed myself from those experiences by jumping from one relationship to the next. From 16 years of age, I had always been in a relationship, and I did not know how to be alone. Well over a decade of baggage was taking an unexpected amount of time to loosen and disappear. That night, I learned how important it was to connect with myself because up until then, I had no clue what would truly make me happy without a companion. If you are in a relationship and you have no idea as to what truly makes you happy, aside from your partner, you are missing the true meaning and experience of life. You never should live life depending on an addiction to lead you to happiness. Find the balance and allow yourself to remain balanced. I thought to myself, how can I fill this void properly, if I do not know what really makes me happy? I needed answers and guidance as to what was going to happen next in my life.

By now, I had denied myself male companionship, any and all communication with my ex, and even put myself on restricted social access with the world. I even went on a solo vacation, as an initiation to my new focus. When I denied potential male encounters, most found it strange. Clearly, I was alone and dealing with some things, and a lot of men tried to prey on that saying, "It looks like someone hurt you, but if you give me the chance, I can make it all better." They thought it was strange for me to be traveling all alone and simply doing everything by myself. I was not cocky with it, though. I did not make them think that I was on some male-bashing spree preaching, "I'm an independent woman and I don't need a man," because I wanted a man and I wanted to depend on my man, too. I just wanted to depend on the type of man who was compatible with me, after healing, and when I was at my best, not some desperate man in need of a good time or who would feed off my vulnerability. I was not ready for the type of man that I needed to complement me, because my judgment was still off track. What I thought could be a good prospect at that time was probably not. Seems to me that a good prospect would want a good catch, and I was far from being considered a good catch. Therefore, the best choice for me was to regretfully turn both the good and bad prospects down. I was not the same person, and through all of the tossing and turning of my emotions, now I was humble enough to allow the natural forces of healing to take place. I managed to survive

Learning the New You & Finding Your True Value

my days, weeks, and months, but now it was time to study this new woman I had become, and rebuild her value. When I prepared for change and detoxified my focus, I was in the purging stages of healing. After detoxifying, I was left with a void that had left me questioning myself with, "What's next?" It was time to search for my true value and set goals based on my new focus.

In earlier chapters, I explained that when you get out of an addictive relationship, you adopt good and bad habits from your situation. Now that you are focused on ridding yourself of the bad habits, you need to find out what makes the person you are now, happy. You must keep in mind the addiction is not an option to keeping you happy. Whatever makes you happy should not drastically change your mood if it is taken away. You need to find your own values based on what you want and the new you. It is important that you know who you are as an individual; otherwise, how would you know what you truly want? This chapter will focus more on you, and learning everything about you as a new individual. This is a beautiful moment in your life, because you will open the door to the new and exciting adventures that are all inside of you. In this stage of healing, you will find out things that you did not even realize about yourself!

The only way, really, to exhaust your possibilities is to get out and try to do as much as you can, keeping in mind that you are only looking for what interests you the most, without giving in to the addiction. While detoxifying your focus, you should have taken yourself out and dined at restaurants, shopped for new gifts, and even taken pictures of yourself throughout your progress. By doing all of these things, you should have formed new attractions to the new things you like, and grown aware of the new things you don't like. Finding out what you like should not be a replacement, but something entirely new. You are still learning the importance of being a strong individual. After a breakup or breakaway, your emotions are in critical condition and you are in an ICU (Intensive Care Unit) of healing. You don't go from the ICU to everyday activities in a matter of days, and so it is the same for your emotions and flesh. You have to care enough about yourself to give yourself the time to heal properly. Our goal is to find pure contentment and happiness within ourselves, before we decide to explore the world. You need to hone this understanding on your terms before you outsource, otherwise you can get caught up in the wrong force. Learning about the new you and finding your true value will take time, depending upon how complex you are, and these two methods work hand in hand with each other. In order to find value within yourself, you have to understand why it is valuable to you. Once you understand the new you and why you do the things that you do, then you will be able to place value on your own attributes. After going through all of this hard work, you will definitely find value in your efforts. In finding value, you will not tolerate anything less than self-respect, and that is how you build your confidence. You will subconsciously demand respect in everything you do and even say. You will learn to be the boss of your emotions and desires instead of *it* being the boss of you.

Learning the New You & Finding Your True Value

ADMIRING YOURSELF

Look at yourself in the mirror and take pictures if you have to. I know this may sound a bit conceited and vain, but trust me, it works! Think about dancers; they have to practice in front of mirrors in order to see their progress as they shape and transform their bodies into the right positions to perform the right moves. The same concept applies when you look at yourself. The purpose of looking at yourself and studying your every move is to get a better perspective of you, but from a different outlook. Have you ever been able to solve someone else's problems, but when it came to your own problem, you were clueless about how to fix it or get through it, and so you called someone else for advice? Often, it is easy to see the solution when looking at other people's problems, and then give them advice. The solutions are so simple to you because you have the ability to look at the problem without being blinded by emotions and circumstance. The fact of the matter is that you are looking at the problem from the outside in. When the problem belongs to you, your view is from the inside out. From this perspective, you may not see how your actions could have provoked the problem, and you can not see your actions until you reflect on the situation from a broader perspective, at least initially.

Literally, look at you in the mirror, think about the situation at hand, and help yourself with your own issues. By constantly looking at yourself, and your every move, you begin to view yourself from the outside looking in, because you have a physical visual, just like you would when you are giving advice to someone else. Make faces in the mirror based on your mood. This is what others see, and through learning you, you need to know what you portray to others. Do whatever you need to do to get to know you better inside and out. As explained previously, take pictures of yourself. Every time you take a picture, you should remind yourself of how you feel at the moment. Take another picture, a little later, and compare the pictures. Look into your eyes, and look at the expression on your face. What is different in those pictures? Did you feel different when you took the pictures? Stay vigilant to yourself the same way you would to anything else you were trying to understand completely. Taking pictures and looking at yourself are amazing ways to get to know the person everyone else knows so well. That person is you from the outside looking in.

Learning Yourself

If you study yourself, you will discover things about yourself that can reveal the reasons behind why you do some of the things you do. If you search deep within you, you truly will learn who you are. When I say search deep within, what I mean is that you need to pay close attention to yourself. Sit quietly by yourself and spend some time with you, alone. You should be able to answer the following questions about yourself, and your family, because we are all the offspring of someone. If you cannot answer these questions, it would be very beneficial to your healing to find them out.

- Where did your family come from?
- Who made you, shaped your character, and influenced your behavior?
- What are/were the challenges of your parents?
- What are/were the challenges of your grandparents and great-grandparents?
- What are/were the challenges of their offspring?

Learning more about your family tree will bring light to your circumstance. You may find that one of your family members struggled with an addiction, or that they learned how to overcome this addiction. You will also realize that nothing is new under the sun. Dig into your history and find out the actions of your grandparents and great-grandparents and their offspring if you can. You never know, it just might work for you. Either way, getting to know more about your family totally will help you in your quest to getting to know the new you after having come out of such an experience. Do the research and find out what you are made of.

What is your blood type? Are you allergic to anything? If you are, do you know why? All of these things make up you, so you should understand them. The things that make you affect the way you feel, react, and operate. Did you know that once you figure out your blood type, you could find out what exercise best fits your needs of becoming a healthier you? I recommend that you get books or videos, which can help you to understand yourself better. After learning my blood type, I researched and discovered that I needed to feed myself certain foods, especially when I am dealing with certain emotional mood swings. It also helped me optimize good health according to my blood type. When you are healthy, you make better decisions and feel livelier. It is imperative that you know what foods work best for your blood type, because different foods affect how well your blood functions in your body. That research drove me to understanding many other elements to improving my mood, and the person I am over all. You can learn so much when you just spend time getting to know yourself.

I'm the type of person who does not like to feel limited, and I live my life in this manner. I constantly plan and forecast my future ahead of time. My mind is consumed with planning for my future and making sure that I will not to fail at those plans through diligent focus. I almost always purchase everything in duplicates, if I can, in an effort not to run out of anything. After spending some time with myself, I discovered why I had grown to be this type of person without ever realizing it. Growing up with five siblings, we ran out of necessary items more times than I would care to remember. It annoyed me tremendously and that experience planted itself inside of me. We would run out of stuff like milk, so I could not eat my cereal unless I ate it dry or with water. We would run out of soap, so I had to use shampoo or dishwashing liquid to bathe. We would even run out of toilet paper, but I won't get into that alternative. I could go on and on about the things we would run out of, but I think you get my drift. The point is, those experiences from childhood made me never want to run out of anything again, if I

Learning the New You & Finding Your True Value

could help it. So, when I was old enough to shop for myself, I started purchasing in bulk or duplicates. People who do not know me, including myself at one point, can perceive that part of me as being greedy or selfish. Had I not reflected on my true feelings and myself, I would not have the slightest clue as to why I subconsciously grabbed at least two of everything, or purchased items in bulk. It could even have a little to do with my zodiac sign, as I am a Libra and crave balance. Whatever it is for you, be sure that you research it and find out. You do not want anyone else to know you better than you know yourself. If someone else can convince you of who you are, then they can convince you that you are incapable when you are capable; that you are *not* valuable when you are invaluable, and the list could go on. Discovering your true value means knowing your value and never allowing anyone else to tell you better about yourself. You should know you best!

Be aware of how you come across to others. Pay attention to everything you do, but most importantly, why you do it. Understand what emotion sparked your action or feeling. This will take some inner soul-searching. If everywhere you go, people tell you that you talk loudly, or you are extremely rude, then most likely you are a loud-talking, rude person. Whether you believe it or not, you may not even realize it. If everyone tells you that you are lazy, then maybe you should take a look at yourself to see if you are really lazy. I know, most people say, "Don't mind what other people think," but I only agree to an extent. That extent is where you disagree because you don't want to face the truth. All I am asking you to do is address your behavior and check all of those bad habits. At the end of the day, it will make you a better person and pleasant company for other people to be around. These suggestions will force you to learn yourself and be the best person you could possibly be. Remember, if you want the best, you have to be your best.

Don't act in a rage because something isn't going your way; that is the behavior of an undisciplined kid. Remember, you are disciplined now; therefore, by default, you understand there are certain ways to conduct yourself and more importantly, express yourself. This will take time, but with perfect practice it will become second nature.

SEXUAL APPETITE

I knew a girl who had grown so addicted to pornography that she naturally had become drawn to people who were sexually explorative. Please, for the sake of your appetite, soul, and health, do not *feed yourself* pornographic material. This too can become an addictive dragon, which will lead you down a path that can be very detrimental to your relationships, nature, and life, just as it was to this girl. Her explorative nature brought about more addictions, and she became promiscuous with many different partners, which later ended her up in the hospital and emotionally exhausted. Her sexual appetite wanted more and more; every time she would satisfy one craving, she was craving for the next. She depended on contraceptives and condoms to save her from her dangerous lifestyle, but they did not. It caught up with her when she discovered she had developed cervical cancer due to a disease called Human Papilloma Virus (HPV). She had contracted HPV during her promiscuous phase, but she had no idea she had it, because there were no symptoms to warn her about this disease.

Did you know that men **cannot** be tested for HPV, and yet they are the ones who carry it and transfer it to women? This virus is very serious, and research shows that it is the leading cause of cervical cancer in women. In 2007, the American Social Health Association (ASHA) – HPV Resource Center reported that about 75-80% of sexually active Americans will be infected with HPV at some point in their lifetime. So that means at least 7 out of 10 sexually active people will have had HPV at some point in their life; that is ridiculously high. The ASHA also reported that, by the age of 50, more than 80% of American women will have contracted at least one strain of genital HPV. The bad part about this disease is that there is no cure, and some people think it is rare because they do not hear about it all the time. Don't wait until you contract something before you start caring about your health. Imagine that; it is becoming even harder for people to practice sexual promiscuity. Perhaps sex was not intended to be treated so loosely. Have you ever thought about where sexually transmitted diseases came from? We pay the price for our sexual immorality with disease, and I think the institution of marriage suffers because of this growing epidemic. Once we all realize just how valuable our body is, gambling it to please the flesh or because we feel that we owe someone something will become an unreasonable exchange. Let us go back to when we were pure and innocent. Just because you are no longer a virgin does not mean that it is too late to guard, protect, and secure your value.

Sex has been so polluted with immorality that it does not appear to be sacred anymore. It's as if sex has become a simple pleasure to ease an urge. Like when you get hungry, you eat; when you are horny, you have sex. These days, sex comes before love. What happened to the love? What happened to the chase? Now, it seems as though the common practice is that you meet your partner, have sex, get to know each other, and, if you get lucky, fall in love last. When sex is treated like an itch that needs to be scratched, I think it enables compulsive desires and condones a lifestyle contrary to a healthy monogamous relationship; and I believe you devalue your worth.

We should hold sex with the highest regard and view it as a special gift, especially because it can be detrimental, and cause havoc to our bodies if abused. As a responsible individual, a more personal suggestion would be to condition yourself to live up to standards that value your own worth, in order to view sex in a sacred capacity. You do not have sex to fall in love. You fall in love and then have sex, because sex is a way to unite the love you should already have. You cannot think that having sex will make, or form, love, if it is not already established, because it won't. I believe that we are selling ourselves short if we think that just because we like someone a lot, they deserve our body. That type of behavior does not value self-worth. Trust me, when you start living up to the standards you set for yourself, you will start attracting the people that are like you. I'm celibate, and I have attracted friends, both men and women, who share the same values, and we respect each other's principles. Believe me, there are people out there that truly value themselves, and yes, men are included in this category, too. Not all men are the same; please understand this. I did not start attracting people who valued good morals until I became the type of person who cared enough about me to guard the vessel and body I live inside. You only get one body, and disease does not care about your age or looks. Just because you may be young, do not think you have time to get it right. You must get it right, right now! Don't disappoint yourself in the future because you thought you were young and could afford to make mistakes. That is not valuing your worth, and you will regret it.

FINDING YOUR TRUE VALUE

Now is the time to go out and accomplish all of the things you ever wanted to accomplish. You will find value in all of your efforts. Primarily, focus on bettering yourself. Go back to school, or complete that project you have been working on for years, or have been meaning to complete. When you finish what you start, you will see that it will encourage you to do more great things. This book had been on my heart well before I met ex number three, but I was so emotionally tangled that I could not allow my creative chemistry to produce what my heart wanted to express. I only was keeping myself in chains, hoping to find contentment. Once I loosened myself from my addiction, and really worked on my value, I produced this book, which I never thought I would ever complete. There is not a person in this world who can tell me that I am not valuable or good enough because I have planted the seed of greatness inside of me, and it has become part of my foundation. That is exactly what needs to happen while you are in the stage of revitalizing the new you.

Go to the gym! Let your outer being be a reflection of your new inner being. Remember, exercise releases chemicals in your brain that give you a feeling of vitality. While you physically rid yourself of the extra baggage, you also increase your value by showing yourself that you care enough about you to take care of the vessel in which you live. You also add years to your life by staying fit. Did you know that some gyms even offer free childcare services while you are working out? Normally these are the larger, more established gyms, but research your local gyms and find out. Don't let the responsibilities of children hinder you from getting a good workout. Take them with you if you have to. Children have a way of bringing out the best in you. They are so innocent, lively, and full of healthy energy that you just may need to keep you going. When you see how much your child needs you to survive, you will realize just how valuable you are.

Research the right food for your body, and start feeding your body the foods it needs to function at its best. During my health research, I discovered the importance of having an alkaline body. Did you know that when you have an alkaline body, it energizes your life? Studies have shown that by having an alkaline body, you can avoid many illnesses. If you want to make your body more alkaline, do your research on alkaline foods and water ionizers. When you research water ionizers, you will find that it is marketed as a potent antioxidant for the body, which can slow aging and prevent diseases. When you open your eyes and focus on your self-worth, you are opening the door to higher standards for your life. Prove to yourself that you are valuable to you by following through with all of your goals, and stay healthy while you do it. Everyone around you will feel your new glow. When you find your purpose, you have found your treasure chest. Finding your true value is searching from the inside and working your way out to better yourself. You must elevate yourself mentally, emotionally, physically, spiritually, and socially. You have to be your best if you want the best!

GOOD EFFORTS ARE NEVER MADE IN VAIN

A friend of mine was having some issues with her husband. He worked out of town, and spent about 75% of his time away from home. The original agreement was for him to work one year out of town, and then he would have to return home. Her husband was approaching his third year of working out of town, and she was beginning to feel the strain of being a single mother. If she tried bringing up the topic of her husband returning home, he somehow would make her feel guilty for desiring such a thought. She began to feel as if her husband enjoyed spending all his time away from home. She also began to feel as though he was seeing someone else, and his old behavior was starting up again. It was always difficult for her to express herself to her husband, because he would shut her feelings out, or make her feel as though she complained too much. She got to the point where she did not want to push her husband away, and so she put all of her anxiety and feelings on the back burner so as not to disrupt her family or husband's mood. She was at his mercy, but did not have a way to vent and express herself from an adult perspective, away from kids. She had abandoned her career and became a domestic housewife and mother. All of her time was spent caring for her home and family, and interacting with her kids, and she longed for adult interactions with her husband, but he was absent. She began to feel undervalued and insignificant, because no one, including her husband, cared about her feelings, or appreciated her work.

Finally, she got fed up and decided to present her concerns to her husband in hopes that he would understand and be more than willing to come home and lighten her burden. She expressed how desperately she needed him to come home because she missed his companionship and support. She even explained how it was critical that she express herself on an adult level regularly, instead of with kids all the time. She told him that she felt like a single mother and wanted him to come home so they could feel like a family again. Agitated by her request, her husband found a way to paint her

Learning the New You & Finding Your True Value

feelings as unreasonable and called her ungrateful. Eventually, her concern turned into an argument, and he just hung up the phone before coming to a resolution. She hated ending phone calls in this way, and her husband knew it. One week had passed, and she still had not heard from her husband, despite her several attempts to contact him. At this moment, she felt hopeless; her husband did not want to come home. Now feeling distraught and lifeless, she decided to send him an email saying that she was fed up, and was tired of his traveling and being away from home. She reiterated how unwanted and insignificant she felt to him. She thought no one appreciated her. She sealed her email by writing, "Maybe if I was dead then I'd get some attention for at least a day or two." She felt suicidal because she could not find a reason to live. When she showed me her email, I immediately rebuked those feelings of suicide, and I knew that I needed to help her find her true value. I saw her value: She had three beautiful children to live for, was a loving person to everyone who came in contact with her, and was simply inwardly beautiful. She had gotten so fed up with her husband, and felt as though she had nothing because he was barely home. She felt that he was not providing her the same respect, or putting her on the same pedestal on which she'd put him.

Regardless of your problems, I still stand strong in my belief that when you know your worth, suicidal thoughts are eliminated from your options and you know better than to resort to such a decision that leads to your demise. You know that you are way too valuable to even sink that low into depression, because your value simply will not allow it. It was clear that she had lost focus of her true value. You should never allow a person to define who you are, or how valuable you are. This is something you have to hone on your own. My friend could not see that because she was so wrapped in her problems, and losing her self-worth and value. I had to remind her how remarkable she was at being a faithful mother, and loyal wife to her husband, even when times got rough. Aside from remaining loyal to the commitment she had made to God through holy matrimony, she was a remarkable person, as an individual. She actually held her family together and did an awesome job at it. At that moment, she thought that all of her work was done in vain, but I could see that it was not. I told her that she should be very proud of herself, and that if she persevered through this time in her life, her sacrifices would not be in vain. I told her never to allow the adversary to steal the glory she had earned through obedience, by falling into despair. I told her to cry it out, but not with tears of anguish, instead with tears of faith, knowing that a higher power has the authority to deliver us from emotional agony. I began to cry tears of joy as this message flowed through me. I expressed to her that prayer changes things, and if she could not pray, I would pray for her. Though I could pray and hope for her, one thing I could not do was believe for her. That goes for everyone in this healing process: You have to believe in your own faith, and allow it to strengthen you. Once you are of good strength, you will have the power to do one of the hardest things in the world: change and maintain your value. No

Learning the New You & Finding Your True Value

matter how sad you get, understand that finding your value will open the gates to an unlimited supply of happiness.

MAKE YOU HAPPY FIRST

One of my brothers finally met a very nice woman, whom he considered pursing as a potential love interest…until one day, he was completely turned off by a conversation they had. He was slightly disappointed, but was more relieved that she had revealed information about herself during that conversation. While she thought she was simply expressing her desires for my brother, she really was expressing her self-worth, or lack thereof in his eyes. She told my brother that she was ready to pursue a relationship with him and explained that, before him, she could not find happiness, and that he was the light in her day. She further explained that he was the only one to put a smile on her face, which was not there before. My brother responded by telling her that if she was not happy before him, then she was not ready for him. He explained to her that she was a good woman, but she shouldn't look for a man to put a smile on her face. He believed that true love meant loving someone more than you love yourself. He concluded that if she did not know how to love herself, then she could not even begin to genuinely love anything or anyone else, including him. He told her not to put so much into love, at first. He felt that if she experienced true love for the first time through meeting him, then she should utilize that experience to optimize the love she needs to have for herself first.

Otherwise, he was afraid that the feelings would fade away because she would not know how to maintain what she felt or keep him happy when the infatuation stage faded away. My brother firmly believes that when someone is looking too hard for love, they usually will end up with a broken heart.

    He told her to look for someone to brighten the beautiful smile she already should have and to enhance the joy she should already feel. For instance, he explained how he visits the movie theater alone all the time and thoroughly enjoys his outing every time. Having his friend sitting beside him should only enhance his enjoyment. Whether the friend joins or not will not make or break his experience, because he would still enjoy the movie. A relationship should not make or break you; it should only enhance you.

    After listening attentively to my brother, I asked him to shed a little more wisdom from a healthy male's perspective. I preferred hearing the advice of a healthy male, with no ulterior motive. He later explained that in valuing yourself, and through learning the new you, you should set your standards of self-worth by the way you treat yourself. He felt that the advice, "Find a partner who will treat you better than you treat yourself, if not better," was flawed to some degree. The main flaw in this concept, according to my brother, was that most people do not know how to treat themselves. He said most people treated themselves generically. "Having material things doesn't mean you are treating yourself on platinum status. It just means you look good. Fake gold, platinum, and cubic zirconium, as well as silver-plated jewelry, all look good, but it all fades over time. If a person was wearing a platinum diamond ring worth thousands, and I asked to borrow it, I'd most likely get laughed at," exclaimed my brother. "But most people give up something that is supposed to be worth more than platinum and diamonds with ease or in a matter of days. That isn't holding you in high regard, or with great value; that's being generic." When people can learn how to truly love themselves, and find the joy and pleasure within without depending on another, then they are truly whole. Now, they have what they need to share themselves with a person worthy of having a long, happy relationship.

Finding what fulfills you and learning why it fulfills you is one of the best ways to realizing your happiness. I really gained some great insight listening to my brother, because it made perfect sense to me. Why is it that some people think it is impossible to be happy before you secure a mate? I hope your own company is not that bad to be around; if you feel it is, then this is the time to change. Knowing what fulfills you will allow you to guard exactly what you feel is important to you.

Living life to the best of your ability is not about being rich. Living life to your best ability is about freedom, independence, and taking control of yourself and planning your future. Therefore, be sure to make a plan, and be your own rock as you venture off to build your own happiness.

WOUNDED *by* BETRAYAL

VALUING YOUR WORTH

Breaking away from an addiction and then going right back to the same addiction can have a toll on you. Once you value your worth, it will be easier to dismiss the possibility of going back to old habits. I remember when I was trying to break away from my exes; I went through some major challenges every time I would go back. Though they did not ask for me to come back, I knew the door was always open if I wanted to go back. This is sort of how addictions work for the rest of your life. If you feel the temptation to go back, then you need stop and redirect your drive. You have to find your self-worth in order to shut the door and never go back.

I know there is no perfect person, so when I refer to "perfect" in the following paragraphs, I mean perfect for you.

Many of us want the "perfect companion," yet we are not prepared to handle the "perfect relationship." We are not even ready to be the perfect companion for a relationship. Do you think the "perfect companion" deserves someone who does not realize their worth, or is still addicted to an old ex? Essentially, it would mean there is lingering residue from the past. Until you rid yourself of your past hurts and value your worth, all you are doing is expecting more than you actually can take care of. It isn't wise or responsible to expect something for which you can not properly care. I was faced with this realization when I went through my angry withdrawals and questioned why I could not just be happy with a companion. Realizing I had not valued my worth and knowing that

Learning the New You & Finding Your True Value

it would take time to do so was a hard pill to swallow. I did not want to hear *wait*; I wanted instant gratification and ease. I had to accept that I needed to first prove I could care enough about me, so I could prepare myself for my blessings. I knew that as long as I considered going back to any of my exes, when I knew we were not compatible, showed me that I was not standing up for my self-worth. Standing up for you, and caring enough to wait, is the only way you will be able to transform yourself into perfection, assuming you want to attract perfection. In order to find happiness, you need to stand up against the battle of doubt and fear, then trust and believe in yourself enough to build yourself back up. The sooner you realize your worth, the better the experience will be on your journey through healing. Don't be afraid to go through emotional discomfort to find your value, because the most important value you can treasure is loving yourself. When you make it to this stage of healing, giving into temptation will not be an option. When you respect yourself on this level, you reap great benefits and radiate confidence. Your confidence will become a protective shield, which radiates protection all around your being.

Let me rewind for a moment, to the breakup/makeup/breakup phase with ex number 3. During those days, I was highly concerned with how I always went back to him. I was confused as to if he ever would be the right person for me. I diligently prayed for us to be together even though I knew he were not compatible. Even while praying I felt guilty, as if I was selfishly requesting favor for something that was not right for me. Though I thought I was doing the right thing, by asking in prayer, I soon realized I was praying selfishly. I was praying for what the flesh wanted, and the flesh wanted my addiction, but obviously that was not healthy for me. Instead, I should have been praying for deliverance, peace, and harmony in my life. I had a lot of work to do on myself. Eventually, I came to the realization that I needed to pray for strength to mold myself as if I was preparing to be the bride of Christ. I felt that in doing that, then, and only then, I would value my worth, and position myself to receive the companion ordained for me. I came to the conclusion that only through God would I find the perfect man, because without God, there is no perfect man. The reason my exes were not the right partners for me were, partially, the same reason I was not the right person for them. We were not equipped to handle all the necessary duties of a healthy, lifelong, and committed relationship. Any attempts to get back together were destined to fail because we were trying to do it our way. We never went to God for the healing our relationship needed. We both needed to devote ourselves to the truth, which was God, and then ask to be united through truth, love, and happiness, if we were really supposed to be together.

With this awareness, I had no choice but to continue my healing process. I was convinced that the only way for my companion to find me would have to be through God, if I was that important to him. It was hard, really hard to accept this, but the truth normally is always hard to accept. I knew that if my "perfect" partner did not go to God for me, he never would find me, even if I were standing right in front of him. I knew this because my eyes had been opened to the truth. The same truth went for me, too; I had to go to God for my "perfect" partner. This left me with a lot of preparing on my part. When you trust in the truth, and go to God for guidance, you still will be happy if, at the end, you do not end up with the person you thought you were supposed to be with. By doing it the right way, you find peace in the outcome, regardless of whether it was not what you expected. You will realize that you are walking down the path set out to make you the best you can be. If it really was meant to be after all of the hard work you put in, you will meet each other again. If not, then you have not yet met the one who deserves you, and is meant for you. I would not have it any other way. After all, I know who I belong to, and I only want what is ordained for me. If you try to make something work on your own, out of the interest of your flesh, it will not have substance or longevity. The flesh is like our emotions, erratic and unstable, and will transform with the slightest of change. Until you learn your lesson and value your worth, it will be very difficult to find the right person for you. When I began to value my worth, I knew I had a spiritual obligation to obey the teachings of wisdom, through discipline. This was some journey. When you begin to value your worth, you start to notice that everything around you will change to include your expectations.

PLACING VALUE ON YOUR HARD WORK

Elevate yourself and do things that will compliment you, and your new value. You have come a very long way to diminish your value and progress for just anything. Your experience alone entitles you to maintain the value you just have realized, and worked hard to improve. You should not be obtained easily, because it should take a person who understands discipline to have the new you. Put yourself on that pedestal. By weathering your storm, you now understand that you are far too valuable to settle for a person who does not feel as though he should work, and put in the time, for you. You will no longer give yourself away in the name of depression, or due to a lack of willpower. Anything worth having is worth working hard for, so hold true to that statement. Any person willing to work for you should be willing to work with you to keep you. He will value you because you have valued yourself. He will hold on to you because he has invested in you and has firsthand experience on what it took to win you over. You then become an accomplishment, and a prize he can be proud of and take care of. If you are not worth the hard work to him, why should he work hard for you? When you accept someone, or something that does not have your best interests at heart, you cause turmoil within yourself. Remember, commitment and values go both ways.

Recap

As you continue to build yourself, embrace your healing, make yourself happy first, and capitalize on your true value. Detoxifying your focus clears a space for you to focus on building your true value. Your healing is happening as you read through this book,

Learning the New You & Finding Your True Value

because through awareness, you begin to heal your greatest assets, which are your mind and heart. You should really be feeling excited right now, because you are transforming into the person you were meant to be. You are almost halfway through your healing, but before we move on to Chapter 5, let us revisit our progress so that we visually can keep our focus on the prize.

Progress Report:

- Admire yourself.
- Learn and understand yourself from the inside and out.
- Curb and tame your sexual appetite.
- Hone your true value.
- Never give up on good efforts, because they will pay off.
- Make you happy and healthy first.
- Value your worth and hard work.

Now, let us continue to grow as we enter into the next chapter of healing.

Chapter 5, here we come!

CHAPTER 5

Caution
Empty Pursuits & Empty Promises

WHAT IF?

*L*et's be real for a moment! With all the preparation, focus detoxification, and realization of your true value, ask yourself: What if my addiction could be managed, and my ex pretended to be exactly what I always have wanted? Be honest; after all we're all human. Seriously, let's hypothetically say that your ex approached you and surrendered to all your needs, then promised to give you exactly what you have always desired. What would you do?

- Would you immediately entertain the proposition, forgetting all that you have just gone through, to rely on your partner's word?

- Would you go back, without first looking at the heart of the matter, under the pretenses that this time it is different because you have changed and you are stronger?
- Would you first ask for some type of sacrifice/collateral, to see if it is a serious proposal, just in case it is another trick to tear you down?
- Or would you not even consider the possibility and continue moving forward?

I asked this question to a girlfriend of mine who was trying to get through her breakup. She actually boasted that she wished her ex would try contacting her so she could turn his "ass" down. Guess what? He did contact her, and guess what she did? She secretly got back with him. When I finally found out, she laughed, exclaiming, "Don't you say anything!" I had no intention of saying anything because I knew that breaking away was a process. I also knew that she only was interested in taking shortcuts and using her surface strength as a fuel to keep her strong. She was talking confidently when she thought he did not want her. The moment he decided to pick her back up, she was waiting like a shameful addict on the corner, looking to get her next fix. She knew in her heart that this guy had not changed, but quickly forgot all about the pain she had previously endured. Ask yourself, when will the last time be the last time? At what point do we recognize that change is vital?

Caution Empty Pursuits & Empty Promises

Her strength was only surface deep, which made all that talk just a show. Beneath the surface, she was not really healing, or even listening to herself. She did not put up a fight for herself, and she certainly did not look at the heart of the matter before running back. She did not even ask for collateral or assurance to prove that this time he would sacrifice anything for her. Look at your relationship as an investment. If your partner is *not* willing to invest in you as a true asset, *you* are simply investing in a liability, and your partner becomes the liability to your heart. Anytime you deal with your heart, be sure you are investing in secure assets. Remember, you are building your life, not just going with the flow, and living each day for the fun of it. With all the challenges and potential setbacks life will throw at you, you have to take it seriously.

The harder you work and prepare, the stronger the force that attempts to tear you down will be; however, you have to prepare for it. Build a strong foundation for yourself, and make sure you believe in it enough to stand firm for it, because you *will* be challenged on it. Yes, people do change, but people also pretend to change. When you deal with the heart of a matter, you will be able to distinguish what is real and fake. If you know in your heart that the person has not changed, do not entertain him and throw away all that you have worked for, for empty promises, lest you cast your pearls to the swine. You should not be obtained easily or devoured.

Empty Pursuits

You will know you are being fed with empty pursuits if your partner finally contacts you, but can not figure out how to say anything with substance. Trust me, when it is a pure desire, they will not be at a loss for words. It never fails, just when you think you have it all under control, you will be tempted to stray. I, too, was tempted with empty promises and empty pursuits, all in one attempt, and I chose the fourth bullet of what ifs. This time it had been over five months since the breakup with ex number three. At first, I was strong and felt ready to face the world because I had gone through months of internal healing and training by guarding myself. I had mastered my actions and denied myself any contact with my ex. However, this was easy, considering he was not making any attempts to contact me. I basically had fought my own willpower without an outside force to stand up against. What I did not take into account was how strong I would be if he tried contacting me. As soon as you start doing well for yourself, or your ex notices that you can live without him; it seems as though that is when he will become a little more interested in what is happening in your world.

Ex number three acted out of character by contacting me out of the blue. I actually was surprised at his attempts. His first attempt was an email ordering me to contact him. I deleted it! A few days later, he sent another cocky email, explaining that I was wrong for not even acknowledging his email. His message completely disregarded compassion, remorse, or finesse, for that matter. This was no way to win me over; it only pushed me away even more. Deleted again! Then he tried calling, but I never picked up. At first, I did not even have a desire to respond to the emails or pick up the phone. However, he did not stop; he took it a step further and decided to contact me at work. I was annoyed on many levels because he was taking the disrespect to another level. It was one thing for him to call me on my personal time, but it's another to call me at work and interrupt my mood in front of people with whom I had to be professional. I did not care to expose my personal issues to my work environment. I knew he was simply trying to play games, because in all his attempts, not once did he state the urgency of his consistent intrusions. He simply was not serious. He had lied, cheated, disregarded my feelings, and then let me go without a fight. I could see that he thought he could force his way back into my life, without an apology or invitation, just to see if he could. That is what you call an empty pursuit.

Empty Promises

You will know you are being fed empty promises when your partner promises things but expects *you* to deliver before the promise is fulfilled. At this point, ex number three had to step his game up, so he resorted to empty promises. Eventually, he cracked my shell and managed to get me on the phone after leaving what sounded like a suicidal message on my voice mail. He really was trying to reach out to me. Not thinking, I called him back. I was not prepared for any romantic advances. I thought I was simply doing the right thing, trying to reach out and help him in his "suicidal" state. He was never the suicidal type when we were together, just the type to play games. Little did I know that it was another trick to suck me back in, and this suicidal stunt was his game strategy to talk to me.

How did I fall for this one? I have no idea. I guess I did not think he would ever stoop that low. After we talked about his "suicidal" episode, it opened the door to communication. Remember, you have to guard yourself, because the moment you let it down, you will be attacked. I was blindsided. He called again, this time exclaiming that he not only wanted to marry me, but was also ready to do it. He exclaimed that he was ready to start a family and build a home with me. Honestly, in my heart, I could not find the sincerity in his words. I will be honest, though, the pursuit sounded really good, because I had not completed my healing. I decided to see how much he would sacrifice for me, by how well he had thought out his plan to get me back. By this time, words meant nothing to me, because he already had mastered what to say to get me back, after years of my drilling it into his head. At this point, I told him actions spoke louder than words, and this time I chose bullet number three. I explained to him that if he was serious, then he needed to meet me half way. I suggested that he should begin to meet the monetary demands of a family household. My home was already halfway paid off, and so I told him to pay the other half if he was serious about getting married. Planning a wedding could take months, just enough time for him to change his mind. However, paying off the rest of the house was just a click of a button, thanks to online banking. After all, he was not investing in anything that would not be beneficial to him. He wanted my hand in marriage, and I wanted to see if he really would take care of me. I knew paying off the rest of my house would not even begin to break his bank, so my request really was not unreasonable. It was not about money for me. It was about sacrifice. Would he be willing to invest? I did not need his money, and he knew it. However, he had popped back into my life with this drastic proposition, so I returned a drastic demand, except it would not be so drastic if his pursuit were real. When a person is serious about marriage, giving to his partner is just like investing and giving to himself, because you both belong to each other. When taking on the role as a husband, boyfriend, wife, or girlfriend, there is a certain position to be assumed. This position demands precise deliverables, lest you fail at fulfilling your position and losing it all. That is why it is absolutely critical to fully understand this type of commitment, and role before committing; otherwise, over time, it becomes diluted with resentment and eventually fails.

I knew that he would not invest his money in anything he was not serious about. You have to know what you are dealing with if you choose to play this game. If you choose to take this route, be sure that you suggest something you know your partner considers valuable. If ex number three valued the time to go golfing or sitting on the couch watching television all day in his spare time, I would have asked him to sacrifice it for the relationship. You know someone really cares when he is willing to give up anything to gain everything. I was willing to see if he truly had changed, and was prepared to commit his life to a healthy family. He would have gained so much more by this small sacrifice. At the time, he promised to deliver his monetary obligation, purchase the ring, and even asked me to get my old wedding dress sized. I had purchased a wedding dress, a couple of years back, from his last proposal. Then, we actually made it to Las Vegas to get married, but after I purchased my dress, he talked his way out of going through with the ceremony, and we never made it down the aisle.

The next time I spoke to him, he drastically had changed his tune. It was almost as if I was supposed to forget all about what we had discussed previously. I had done my sacrificing, and to be honest, I did not expect him to deliver, but you know how women can get when it comes to love. We want to see with our own eyes, before we officially cancel out all possibilities. It seemed as though he just wanted to go right back into our same old, routine, rollercoaster relationship. He was expecting me to deliver my time and heart without him delivering his promises. Therefore, I brought it back up and asked several questions: "What about the ring? When are you talking about getting married? What's the proposed wedding date? When are you going to put my name on your bank account? When do I get full access to you? When are you going to tell everyone about your decision?" He was speechless. I continued on explaining to him that marriage was not a joke to me. I told him that I did not think it was fair to dangle empty promises in my face in the hopes of getting me all excited, just to have me in the palm of his hand. Still, he was speechless. He thought that whispering sweet nothings in my ear would pump me up to fall back into routine, as it had so many times before. This time was a little different, and I think he knew it. After my questioning, he simply disappeared and fell off the face of the earth, without answering a single question. Several days passed, and I did not hear from him, but I could see he was posting messages and pictures to his friends' Facebook walls. Were they more important than me? I thought we were planning a wedding. Here I am, supposed to be his future wife, serious business this time, and I do not even as much as get a phone call? I accepted change this time and held him accountable for this pursuit. I called him, and asked why? "Why would you build me up just to tear me down? Do you find pleasure from hurting me? Why haven't you called? Why did you even pursue me in the first place? I was doing just fine by myself all those months, but you just had to call and interfere with my healing. Do you even have the ability to care about an individual? **Why?**"

The only explanation he gave was, "I don't know." To be honest, I did not really need to know the truth. The fact of the matter was that I did not want the leader of my future family confused before the family even got started. However, holding true to the "accountability of actions," I demanded the truth. I told him to try harder and to provide me the truth because I did not deserve this half-assed empty attempt. I firmly asked, "What is the truth?"

Out of the blue, he yelled, "I have a three-year-old child with my ex-wife; do you still want me?" I must say that I never, even in my wildest dream, expected him to say that. He and I were together for five years and had broken up less than six months ago. Therefore, you do the math. This guy held so many secrets; I did not want to stick around to find out the rest. His family did not even know about this mystery child. All I could think was how could he hide his own child for so long? I even wondered if he was telling the truth about this child because he was known to play many games and lie for no reason. He claimed he wanted to change, and it seemed a little unnatural for me to completely walk away without giving him another chance to prove it to me. He also claimed that he was ready to be the man I always wanted, and to love me the way I deserved to be loved. The truth of the matter was that he never had intended on investing in me because I never saw the ring and he never lived up to his promise. It was another ego-boosting game to him. It was my turn to be speechless, because I was in shock.

"Do you still want me?" he asked again.

I soon popped back into reality, and confusingly answered "**no**," but for several different reasons. If he could hide his own flesh and blood from me, there was no limit to his games. Marriage with him would only be the beginning of a nightmare. I did not want to devote my life to a problem, to a man who never respected me enough to tell the truth, just to be a married woman. I did not want to build my foundation on a lie, and I figured there were many more lies attached to him. I realized the obvious truth was that the flame of my love for him had not completely extinguished, for me to consider his attempt. Had I not gone through all that previous healing, I don't think I would have been able to convince myself, even with a million dollars, that I'd be strong enough to say *no* to him, even with the mystery child. Though it felt like I had taken a couple steps backwards by entertaining his empty pursuit, at least it was not 10 steps. That night, I let out a big cry and I was back on my feet by morning. This time, I did not think twice or regret the decision I had made.

Why is it that when you are on the right track, and doing just fine, the enemy has a way of trying to steal your joy by throwing a distraction in your path? It seems that when we pull ourselves up in life, put enough pieces back in place, and start strengthening the inner us, a distraction is thrown to interfere with progress. Routine maintenance is what you should venture to maintain, and be cautious of distractions. Be careful of the empty promises and empty pursuits. Most of all make sure you study just how much you are worth in the eyes of your pursuant. Then ask yourself, are you worth more than how your pursuant values you? If you believe you are worth more, burn the desire to look back and move on.

Be sure that you are able to recognize genuine change. More importantly, remember the cause of the breakup. Don't make the mistake and return out of mercy or pity. Know what you are getting yourself into and the potential setbacks to your emotions, progress, and life. If you consider your ex again, stand firm for your needs. The consideration needs to be made from a logical perspective, one free from addictive indulgences. Pay attention to what he is willing to sacrifice for you, because that will show you how valuable you are in his eyes and heart. Don't just forget about everything you have worked for, and blindly trust his word. Don't take his word at face value either, make him deliver through actions what he is enticing you with words. The proposal should not take a long time to deliver, either. If he was bold enough to step to you with a proposal, then he should be bold enough and able to deliver it on the spot, or at least within 24 hours. Otherwise, it is all empty promises and pursuits.

If you have had enough, and have decided that there are no more chances, even if that person changed, then **kudos** to you! The only words you should have for your ex are: "Great, I'm glad you have changed; now be the best person for the next person." It took me giving my ex several chances and many long, empty nights, before I even was able to reach that milestone. I never gave up, though, and for those who still are fighting, you shouldn't either. Prepare yourself just in case you are approached with empty pursuits and empty promises.

There is nothing wrong with following your heart's desire, but there is something wrong when you disregard what you know is not right for your heart. Take out emotions, take out the flesh, and go straight to the heart of the matter. Cancel out the empty promises and empty pursuits and then ask yourself, should I stay or should I go? What do you deserve? The real question you should be asking yourself, without selling yourself short, is:

Even if this person gave me everything I could possibly hope for and deserve in a relationship...

Would this person truly *deserve me*?

Think about it...

CHAPTER 6

Product of Your Environment

HIDDEN OBSTACLES IN STIFLED GROWTH

Have you ever set a goal for yourself, but found that you were your own setback? It's as if we are our own worst enemy sometimes. It's amazing how we try so hard to get ahead, and even set goals for ourselves, but can not seem to get out of our own way. Who is to blame at this point? Certainly, you want what is best for yourself, but how do you address a lack of motivation after the excitement expires? I'm sure that when you picked up this book, and if you have read up to this chapter, you were, and hopefully still, motivated and pumped up about changing your life. However, what if this book becomes old to you, or everything you have done to make life better for yourself becomes common or just flat-out boring? How would you then sustain motivation and momentum through your journey towards change and healing? What would you live for, if another exciting adventure did not await you tomorrow? I'm referring to the times you probably did not account for, like when your willpower becomes weak or your daily progress feels as though it has slowed down. If you find yourself headed down this road, it is time to switch gears and dig a little deeper for internal contentment. Not to worry, though, because the worst already is behind you.

There could be many hidden obstacles in our daily progress, but we have to remain attentive enough to recognize them. Failed attempts, throughout your journey of healing, could be a result of those unaccounted obstacles. It's common to run into this issue, because hidden obstacles normally live in the foundation of our character. They even can stem from a source embedded in our childhood upbringing. This brings to mind an old roommate of mine who struggled with obesity and wanted desperately to lose weight.

Through her failed attempts, she ended up discouraged and unmotivated. As I watched her habits, day in and day out, it became clear to me why she was not losing the weight, but she had no idea. Her family visited often, and they further revealed to me why she was unable to notice her own habits. She came from a family that conditioned her to maintain a diet high in fat, cholesterol, and sugar. Dessert was a staple to their daily meal consumption, and pork was their meat of choice. She consumed these foods in large portions, and at any hour of the day or night. Her eating habits mirrored her family's diet, but she was unaware that the foods she had consumed all her life had a great deal to do with her weight gain and adult habits. Though she desired to lose weight, she never researched healthy eating habits. To make it worse, she would always initiate her weight loss program by bingeing the day before, as a way of satisfying all of her different cravings. She thought that bingeing was the best way to get it all out of her system, but it never worked. Her plan usually lasted two weeks, at most, before her momentum was exhausted and she decided to give up. She always burned herself out because she focused only on the start and end point, while mentally neglecting to prepare for the time in between. Her lack of discipline to endure patience and perseverance made her goal feel impossible. It made her feel like the time in between was torture, and full of too much sacrifice.

She settled for believing it was impossible to lose weight because she was genetically obese. My roommate had a major flaw in her weight-loss plan, because she never changed her bad eating habits or incorporated exercise into her routine. Instead, she skipped breakfast, and minimized the other meal portions. She thought that she could lose weight if she just starved herself a little. It was not so much portion control as it was what she consumed daily that meant she could not see results. She had never been put on any diet restrictions as a child growing into adulthood. In fact, she was conditioned to eat whatever she wanted, when she wanted. Therefore, whom should she blame for the habits that have been embedded in her lifestyle? I'm sure her family had inherited the same eating habits. Honestly, no one is to blame, except you, when you know better but *choose* not to do better. I'm even referring to those who know something needs to change, but choose ***not*** to explore the possibilities, in hopes of remaining in the dark, and not to be held accountable for knowing better.

We have to get to the bottom of this. Everything you have been exposed to from the moment you were born affects who you are today, and are decisions that provoke your behavior and choices. Like anything that takes time to blossom, the time in between the growing stages can sometimes feel slow and testing. If, when you reach this point of exhaustion, you are tempted to give up or give in, it is important to focus on understanding the dynamics surrounding your temptation. By doing so, you pinpoint why you crave the unhealthy things that constantly appear in your life. Perhaps the cravings stem from the seeds planted in your childhood, seeds you simply did not know had been planted in your foundation or character. By digging into your own background, you unveil those hidden roots, and re-ignite your healing out of its stagnant state. In order to allow discipline to act as a bridge between your goals and accomplishments, it is imperative that you continue believing in yourself and live off of that energy throughout your transformation.

The Generational Cycle of Life

Sometimes you just do not know any better. It is as if your life is on autopilot, and so you coast through life the way you have been

Product of Your Environment

taught. As you aimlessly coast through life, you travel down the same path of your surrounding influences. We have to break the cycle of bondage in this lifetime, in order to make a difference, and make it better for the next generation. Destroying the yoke of bondage connected to our future invites us to live life with an exciting purpose, by creatively steering it in the direction that leads to prosperity and permanent happiness. Positive growth is our focal point throughout this journey. Don't live life only to be accepted by those who are lost themselves. If you also end up lost, then where is the prize or growth in that? Through healing and by living a healthy life, you will be able to recognize those who are lost in bondage. You will also have a better direction on where to gear your desire for acceptance, if it still exists. Many can not even recognize or accept they are living a life of bondage, but without this acknowledgement, it continues to negatively impact our decisions and actions every day. How would you know any better, if you were not exposed to anything else? Your personality and character are influenced immensely by the events you were exposed to growing up. The point is that we are all, to some degree, a product of our environment and childhood. Step outside of your comfort zone and start viewing the different perspectives of life if you really want to grow.

My parents married very young; my dad was 18, while my mom was 15. Back then, and in the South, it was not unheard of to marry young and start a family. In my parents' time, raising a family was thought to be the ultimate prize in life, and so everyone ventured out to find their special someone to build a family with. My upbringing dramatically affected my decision making. It even affected the way I viewed myself and the world around me. My parents raised me in a lifestyle that focused more on the intangible resources of life, which were family unity, and love. My view on life, as a child, dictated my drive and goals as a growing adult. As a child, I thought the main focus to life was securing a husband in order to raise a family of my own. When I thought of becoming a successful adult, a career was nowhere in my sphere of importance. I thought that if I had lost out on the intangible resources of life, I would be losing out everything.

    Don't get me wrong, a strong, close-knit, and loving family still equals success to me today. However, after broadening my views and stepping out into the real world, I have come to understand there are other elements in life that also can equal success, such as knowledge. However, my parents rarely stressed education in the house, because their parents did not expose them to the importance of education. My grandparents came from a generation where education was placed at the bottom of the priority list due to hindrances brought on by widespread discrimination that existed at the time. Their main priority was to work and put food on the table and they believed they did not need an education to do that. As long as they had a skill, and remained employed, they always had the means to feed their family. That is all that really mattered to them, because it sustained love, growth, and happiness. Back then, marriages also lasted "till death do us part." Their practice of survival was passed to my parents, but as time changed, the teachings did not. As a result, I inherited the rooted teachings of my parents' childhood and it molded me into placing more value on the intangible resources of life, rather than college, education, or preparing for corporate America. What do you think happens when you step out into the real world with the indoctrination you have received from home, only to discover most of what you have been taught, including how to love, does not coincide with everyone else's teachings? You find yourself alone, misunderstood, or trying to catch up with understanding what most people place value on. Either way, you will need to find a balance.

    Times have changed drastically. Through the changing of times, we realize just how important education is to maintain stability in life. Education is critical for survival. Good education could open doors to a successful career, but there must be balance. In some cases, we focus so much energy on building our successful careers that we simply forget about love, because it is too hard to manage when combined with a competitive career or lifestyle. We have abandoned love to some degree because it does not put us where society says we need to be. Teenagers and young adults, are not trying to find their soul mates to grow a loving family with anymore. In fact, many young adults will laugh at the thought, because the new times encourage people to play the field before settling down. We are almost fully conditioned to believe that committing to anything serious, in terms of a relationship, will stop us from living life to the fullest.

I have run across several single, young, and older adults juggling potential lifelong partners, who frown at the idea of committing to one person because they feel they need to live life first. It is understandable for a person to explore life as an individual before committing to a serious relationship. However, when did the circle of life, and building a family through committed love become deemed as "not living?" It is become common to see a successfully attractive man, or woman, in their early to late thirties living alone, and unable to find a serious partner with whom to grow. We have almost conditioned ourselves to think that commitment and falling in love is bad for us, and so you see fewer couples respecting loyalty, and more people emotional unavailable. This behavior has resulted in a lack of mass discipline—the kind of discipline that is necessary to commit to one person, or one focus. It appears that being "faithful" has taken a back seat, and if we want to keep up with the current times, following the majority is practical. Now, it is practical to think of only of ourselves in order to move up in status, or obtain the finer things in life, at all costs. We focus more on "getting it out of our system," by experiencing everything that we can possibly expose ourselves to, thereby abandoning discipline and portion control. If we are not careful, what actually can happen is similar to what happened to my roommate. You could grow such a diverse appetite that it can become extremely difficult to control what you crave, thus resulting in your inability to find contentment within yourself or satisfaction in discipline. Getting it all out of your system actually can set you further back. The more we expose ourselves to the unhealthy distractions of life, the greater our fleshly appetite expands. With all the distractions and social pressure nowadays, it is so easy to lose what it really takes to maintain success within our personal lives and hone true love. This includes the love needed to respect you, as well. It is almost as if love does not matter anymore. Where does that put those who desperately crave genuine love? It seems as though we have reached the point where we are chasing love, but do not realize it. Everyone wants to be accepted and loved, but the more we give in to what we think love is, the further away we stray from it. It takes much discipline to maintain and protect genuine love, but we can start by learning to acknowledge the love we must have for ourselves.

Root of the Matter

How would you know that your lifestyle is unhealthy if it is all you have ever been exposed to? How do you know what partner to pick or what to expose yourself to, if you do not know what makes you happy? It would be rather difficult to attempt finding happiness if you do not know what or where it is. How do you know when it is time to let go and move on, if all you crave is commitment to your addiction? In order to answer any of those questions, you will need to learn what specifically nurtures your happiness and why. However, in order to understand exactly who you are and what you need to properly grow, you will need to dig deep into your rooted foundation, and even deeper if you have not yet learned to live your life as an individual. If the common result equals resentment, strife, and failure in your growth, then something is not right for you and you are not growing. You will have to acknowledge responsibility for your own growth and healing. Pay attention to yourself. If you do not acknowledge what it takes to grow, and your actions do not acknowledge what it takes, ask yourself, when will you grow?

Fast forward almost a year into my journey of healing, I had written myself countless love letters, taken myself out on dates, and continued to avoid potential love interests, all in the interest of my healing. I traveled and went on spontaneous vacations all over the world, pampered myself with Thai massages and spa treatments, and enrolled in classes to become a licensed, concealed handgun holder, and motorcycle rider. I hung out with positive girlfriends on "ladies" nights out and celebrated every holiday that passed. I honed my skills by enrolling myself for private gymnastic lessons and joining the local fitness center. I even went as far as learning new and exciting skills by joining a dance organization that teaches the art of pole dancing. I finished my spree of unique exposure by skydiving and jumping out of an airplane at 14,000 feet for the first time, without hesitation. I was so happy during this stage of healing and finding myself, but of course, what goes up, must come down. Even though I had made major progress, I found myself still searching for something more to excite my drive. I thought I was happy and almost completely healed from my past, but my heart still felt the emptiness of despair, even after almost a year of no communication with any old or new romantic interests. It was almost as if I was only healing myself externally. Internally, I still needed to acknowledge some areas that desperately needed healing. Even though I had an amazing journey thus far, I was starting to feel as though my life was slowing down to a standstill because everything I had been doing seemed like it was becoming routine and monotonous. However, I did need all of those exciting experiences to make me stronger and shock me into emotional independence, as it did. I made new memories for myself, too. But even after my adventures, and because I was so focused on getting over the heartbreak, I lost sight, and kind of forgot to focus on my growth.

At that point, I felt as though my progress was headed towards a dead end, because I was confused and did not know what to do next. I was beginning to lack confidence in believing it was possible to heal. All I wanted was for time to pass because I knew that it was the only promising cure. I was afraid that this point of confusion would lead me to simply existing in life, instead of living life. I had forgotten that I needed to continue believing in myself, by finishing what I had started, which was sealing the completion of my healing. It became imperative for me to complete the process, because at almost a year into my healing, I had learned simply to stabilize the pain I was working to heal. Healing and growth was very important to me, because I knew it would close the door to potential relapses. I was fed up with feeling that any of my exes could potentially come right back into my life if they really wanted to. It was as if my door was always open, secretly waiting for that potential comeback. I was also fed up with wondering if I was still a victim to my addiction, especially when I'd hit my low points. I did not want for my adventures to work as a cover-up to the problem. I was serious about getting over this and moving on. I knew I was doing everything right, because I still held true to my morals, and was not guilty of cheating myself throughout the progress. At the beginning of my healing, I decided to remain single and celibate while I sorted through my issues and goals. That meant no dating of any sort. I did not want to confuse, bandage, or distract myself with a rebound or a quick fix. I also wanted to make sure I fully understood myself as an individual before I attempted to share myself in another relationship. I needed to know exactly what I was capable of bringing to the table, by first discovering my own potential and value.

I had made it through my first Christmas, New Year, and Valentine's Day without shedding a single tear of disappointment. I never really expected, after almost a year of the breakaway that I would still need healing, until I slowed down long enough to acknowledge that I could not speed up a healing process that only time and recognition could complete. Pure solitude, learning, and loving myself, the unique adventures, and acknowledging that I still needed healing, all helped me to close the door to resentment and reignite my healing. I knew I had accomplished pushing all of my exes out of my system because I had finally detached myself from any entitlements or hopes of a future with them. I was at peace with the fact that they were simply an experience of the past, a past I now could easily accept leaving behind.

More importantly, in my heart, I wished them all well, but did not feel the desire to follow-up. Just to give you something to look forward to: When you truly leave something in your past, it stops haunting your thoughts in the future.

Even after all of my exciting experiences, I could not understand why I still felt unsatisfied. I had reached the stage where I knew my world could exist without my last ex, I was not bitter or angry, and I truly forgave myself for allowing me to lose myself in the past. However, I still had not found complete peace within. Even though my adventures got me through the most critical part of my healing, which was the pain, I knew it was time to focus more on my internal healing. Whatever was stifling my progress had to be something embedded deeply within me because at that point, there was no reason for me to be disappointed with life. I had no regrets, and I had a fresh start. Through acknowledgment, I realized I needed to revisit the garden of my foundation. I cross-examined my progress to my foundational teachings and future goals. I asked myself:

- Why is commitment so important to me?
- Why do I always feel like a failure if I am not in a relationship?
- Why do I feel as though, deep down inside, I'm still waiting to blossom my career, goals, and life?
- Why did I knowingly continue to subject myself to toxic situations in my past relationships?

After pondering all of my disappointments, it became clear that my unhappiness did not solely stem from the disappointments of my failed relationships, or an unhealthy addiction to clinging to relationships I clearly knew were toxic. Part of the reason I had continued to subject myself to toxic situations in my past was because deep down inside I really wanted my relationships to work out. Unfortunately, I valued that over my own well-being. Then, I looked further into my past, way before relationships, and remembered, as a child, my first understanding of true success was commitment to my family. The seed was planted long ago. Unknowingly, that seed had matured in my foundational garden of life. I realized after all of this time that it was embedded in me to believe my success had to be built in the perfect order of love, marriage, family, and then career. Over time, I added career into that equation but securing a companion to build a family was the first step, with no option of deviation. My growth and success were based from this plan because I was a product of my environment; hence, the ingredients planted in my foundation. If all of this were true, then my core foundation supports that in order for me to find success and begin a "happy" life, first, I had to succeed in building a solid relationship, so everything else could follow. I had just uncovered the root of my unhappiness and finally got to the bottom of my problem by addressing the "whys." That explained:

- Why I held commitment in such high regard;
- The feeling of failure when I suddenly became single;

- My inability to blossom as a single woman; and lastly,
- Why I valued my relationships over my own well-being.

I thought I was working towards the bigger prize by pushing myself aside in my past relationships. I just did not realize that my depth of sacrifice should only be reserved for someone deserving, and not just anybody with the title of boyfriend. It also should have been reserved for someone who would appreciate the value in that level of trust and commitment, and would not take advantage of it just because they could. Deep down inside, I thought that without a life partner, I would not be able to live a fulfilling life. I deferred honing my potential as an individual, and as a woman, by waiting to secure marriage first. Unfortunately, I accepted certain things in my past in order to get closer to marriage, so that everything else would follow through in order. No wonder I was so broken, despairing like a relapsed addict every time my relationships did not work out. My plan for success kept collapsing right before my eyes, and I could not control the failure. Every time my relationships failed, deep down inside, so did my life, and I hated starting over, again and again. Can you imagine rebuilding your career from the ground up every two to six years, just to see it all come crashing down to the ground, for you to rebuild it based on the same hopeful plan? I thought my plan equaled "happily ever after," until I realized that it depended on the commitment of someone else in order for it to work. If my subconscious drove me to believe the plan had to go in that particular order, it meant that I would never find the key to my success if I could not secure a lifetime partner. If that is not ultimate procrastination, I don't know what is. I would never start my life with that kind of understanding hovering over my progress. At this point of my journey, it was time for me to tear down and reorganize my structure. I now understood why commitment was so important to me, and why I felt failure when I would end up single again. The bottom line was that I did not know if I ever would get married at this point. I did not even have prospects, but I had to move on with my life. With this new outlook, I decided to look at my personal life in an entrepreneurial capacity. I could still be happy and successful without a partner. It was sort of like starting my own business, but with a sole proprietorship instead of a partnership. Yes, it would be great to have a partner for added support in the future plans of my business, but it is **not** absolutely necessary for success.

Partnerships are beautiful, but at what point do you draw the line of compromise? Is it when you have been stripped of self-respect, or right before you lose yourself to the undeserving? You can not stop your life because you do not have a partner in it, and you certainly should not abandon discipline just to hold on to a toxic partnership. Business must go on! It takes two like-minded individuals to desire the same kind of success in order to achieve success in a partnership, and that is true for a relationship as well. Your desire for companionship never should override your good judgment.

As you can see, it was necessary for me to revisit my foundational structure. I learned that my last stage of healing had loosened me away from a way of thinking that did not assist in my goal to happiness. At this point of your healing, you have to uncover every skeleton in your closet in order to set yourself free from the bondage of unhealthy setbacks. Releasing your hidden darkness allows the light of healing to shine through. The light of healing will release you from the guilt of protecting any hidden skeletons that would otherwise weigh you down. Of course, my walk is different from yours, but what I am trying to do is help you understand that whatever **your** unique walk may be, only **you** can honestly revisit it in order to get down to the root of what causes your unhappiness. Release yourself from bondage, and for crying out loud, **get out of your own way**! Don't allow negative influences to influence your progress.

COVERING ALL BASES

Perhaps you grew up where you saw someone allow another to mistreat him or her, and through this exposure, a tolerance of acceptance was planted in you that makes you oblivious to being mistreated, mistreating others, or mistreating yourself. Perhaps you grew up where it was common to see couples engage in relationships that involved promiscuity, adultery, lying and cheating. That exposure may have planted an understanding that leads you to question the significance of loyalty, and whether it is even possible. Maybe you grew up in an environment where you were exposed to narcotics at an early age, and now it is planted in your mind that the consumption of any drug is practical. Could it be that you were abused sexually, mentally, or physically as a child, but over the years you have conditioned yourself to forget about the experience, while the experience still dictates your future to a healthy life? Maybe you were abandoned and brought up lacking love in your growth. If any of those stories are yours, you still can recreate your future by acknowledging your past, and clearing out those hidden skeletons. You have to first want to make the change within your life, because no one can do it for you. Without that desire, any attempt of recovering will end in vain, and you will continue to see the same failed results.

Setting standards based on what you have seen, and how you were brought up, is not okay if you were brought up in an unhealthy environment. It is not okay to be mistreated by anyone, physically, mentally, or sexually. Maybe your parent or guardian did not know better. If you have reached adulthood, it is time to stop blaming your past for your current and future failures. Once you reach the age where you can make the change or difference in your own life, the blame falls on you if you choose not to change and succeed. It does not matter how old you are, the fact of the matter is, you never stop growing as long as you live to see another day. Understand that there is always room to grow, live, and learn. Do not focus on the time it will take for you to grow and recondition your life. Instead, focus on the things you need to get you through your daily progress.

We all have been betrayed or let down at some point in our

Product of Your Environment

lives. You should not allow betrayal from the past to disrupt your healing process. It is critical that we address the hurts from our past; otherwise, it will impede future growth. If you dwell on bad experiences from the past, you are, in essence, allowing negative forces to direct your life in the present. Refrain from staying angry at past events, and, instead, focus on transforming your life into one that is emotionally, spiritually and physically healthy. Being healthy on those three levels will enable you to successfully recover from the blow of betrayal, and help you forge ahead, stronger than ever before. Set your standards and live up to good values. Dedication, initiative, and loyalty should be some of the ingredients you plant in your growth, in order to get you through your daily struggles. When you purge yourself of past negativity, you clear your path to a better future.

Positive Figures

After digging deeply into our foundation in search of answers, it is only natural to address the importance of surrounding ourselves with healthy role models, or positive figures, moving forward. If not a role model, then at least someone who will have your best interests at heart when you are in need of direction. You have to continue nurturing your well-being throughout life for continued growth. There are many avenues you can take when securing your own well-being. At one point, I hired a psychologist/therapist to help me sort out the thoughts that were roaming throughout my mind. I needed to make sure that I was not going "crazy" in my fragile state, which seemed to be when temptation tried to utilize my suffering as a way to convince me to give in to unhealthy desires. I also needed someone to bounce my thoughts off of, with an unbiased opinion. Even the therapist encouraged me to keep moving forward in the direction I was headed. I had the answers in the core of my heart, but they were challenged with a force that did not want me to find freedom, which, in the past, made me constantly doubt myself. My therapist encouraged my drive. She listened to me and provided constructive feedback to ponder over. In the end, I was assured that I was on the right track, and was encouraged not to give up. Just remember, you get out what you put in. I highly would recommend that you take the time to invest in your mental health and talk to a professional therapist to help solidify and nurture your current focus. It does not make you crazy or insane to hire someone trained to listen, if you simply need an unbiased opinion or just someone to talk to. It's not expensive at all. It's even covered under some insurance plans. *Do something you have never done before to receive the results you have never had before.*

As you rebuild your foundation and transform yourself from negative setbacks, utilize positive figures to keep you on track and help you find value in what needs to change, from past misguidance. Your positive figure does not have to be a therapist or psychologist. It could be a parent, a friend, a relative, or even your child. Experiences from positive figures should help push you through the most difficult times because they will challenge and encourage you to stay on track along the way. Everyone should have a challenge because challenges force you out of your comfort zone and make you apply yourself in ways that will enhance you. You must surround yourself with healthy people if you want to encourage healthy living.

THE CONCLUSION

You probably will never find a book that outlines how to live life perfectly, but you can utilize your experiences, linked with the time you still have left, to make a difference in your life. My dad always said, "A repeated mistake reflects immaturity, but a learned mistake equals growth." Let us take that a step further: Utilize all of your resources and observe the mistakes of others around you, as well as your own, and then learn from them all. If you are really serious about growing, **stop** making the same mistakes over and over again. Becoming a "product of your environment" should have new meaning by now, because we have learned that we can recreate our own environment. Awareness is where it starts. There are too many examples out there from which to learn. Not knowing and growing up underprivileged is no longer an excuse. You can train yourself to attain whatever you want to achieve in life. If you do not achieve your dreams, it is no one's fault but your own. Therefore, clean up your internal and external environment, and proudly show that you are a product of your "own environment." If you are not willing to address the root of your issues, in order to learn about every element that makes you who you are, then this book will not be able to fully assist you in your growth and future victory. Addictive behaviors are fueled by a lack of discipline and accountability. Maintain discipline by doing the things you know you need to do. Look into your background and root out any unhealthy seeds planted from childhood. Do not live in your disappointments. Instead, learn from them.

Everyone has a conscience that tells them right from wrong. Whether or not you choose to listen to your conscience is solely up to you. What will you choose? Will you choose to listen to your good conscience and abandon your old ways? Will you choose to be strong and stand firm to your new foundation? It is up to you not to allow where you came from determine where you are going? You make your future from here; do not allow your old environment to limit your possibilities. If you don't like what lives inside of you, then change it. It is that simple. Whatever you want to learn, research it and submerge yourself in it. Do not accept or make room for excuses. There is a huge world out there, and you should not limit your growth.

Your improvement in life is a living testimony and will require constant nourishment. As you grow and change, so should your surrounding influences. Get out and surround yourself with those who live the lifestyles you strive to mirror. Don't stand still in the same rut that got you nowhere real fast for all these years. Temptation, during your healing stage, is like the enemy, always seeking to cripple and destroy. Never let your guard down to temptation;

instead, stay vigilant to the distractions that are there to tempt you to stray. Once you heed this awareness, you will be better off with your journey in life. If your idea of healing means looking forward to never dealing with temptation, then you will have a rude awakening. You should view your healing as if you are opening your eyes to the many dangers surrounding you every day. Don't be complacent to temptation because everyone is subject to failure. We all have weaknesses, but they should not be tested in vain, so protect yourself from what you know is unhealthy to your growth. Get serious about your life because life will continue to present challenging battles that you must learn to overcome. Expect the best but prepare for the worst.

Chapter 7, here we come!

CHAPTER 7

Stages of Life
Truly Letting Go

NO REGRETS!

*I*t's written all over your face!" were the words my mom said to me the other day when she revealed her observation of my progress. It was also the first time she openly had commented about my well-being since the initial stages of my last breakup. Well over a year had passed, and little did I know that she was still monitoring the progression of my healing from afar. In the past, she'd randomly inquire about the last time I had spoken to any of my exes, but she stopped asking when my last response was, "Almost a year now, Mom," in that, "I can't believe you are still bringing them up" kind of tone. As I filled my life with positive experiences, the negativity from my past just seemed to drain away. When my past stopped affecting me, I discontinued thinking about it and inadvertently stopped talking about my exes. I did not even notice when I had transitioned into this stage of my healing; it just kind of happened. My mom asked if I had noticed how well I was handling things lately, and then expressed how relieved she was to see that I had finally found stability. Evidently, she too was affected emotionally by my breakup and wanted me to find emotional freedom, just as badly as I wanted it for myself. She said I was glowing, and she knew I was experiencing the joy of victory.

It was not until I stopped anticipating my healing that I actually healed. I was so engulfed with my new life, and learning so much about myself and the world around me; it was as if I had forgotten all about the entire breakup ordeal. Her observation really added perspective to my journey, because at that moment, I realized that I did it! I really did it! I had conquered my addiction, gotten over my breakup, and moved on with my life, all without a rebound to enable those addictive desires. By embracing the healing stages, and allowing them to naturally unfold in my life, I was able to transition into a life that was not dependent on anyone else to fulfill or validate my happiness. I was living, laughing, growing, glowing, and loving again all while remaining celibate, single, focused, and confident. My old life never had felt as free and right as this one. I was missing out on a lot and smothering my growth by subjecting myself to unhealthy attachments. My new life did not have the desire to compromise my happiness by going backwards. I was much stronger, and now was able to make wiser decisions based on what assisted my positive growth, and not what was good enough to feed

Stages of Life—Truly Letting Go

my addiction. I was not desperate for attention any longer. I did not need to compromise just to make things fit in my life anymore because I understood that everything offered to me did not necessarily mean it was for me. I was okay with leaving things that were simply not meant for me alone, and I understood it had nothing to do with whether or not I was good enough for it. I was healthy enough to rationalize my decisions and stick to them based on how they would affect my future, instead of provoking fleshly desire.

A year and a half ago, I was beating myself up over my failure, wondering if I would ever get through the pain from adhering to my untamed fleshly desires. I worried if I would ever find Mr. Right, but right now, none of that matters. What matters to me is remaining healthy and happy as an individual. I'm not worried about not having a partner or a date, companionship, sex, or a family to define me or my success, because the new found energy in my life sustains me. I wake up every morning, excited about my new challenges for the day, and am encouraged to achieve a new goal. I have learned to enjoy every stage of my life because each stage introduces me to growth and allows me to live life optimally.

Looking back on my experiences, I understand why I went through some of the things that brought me to where I am today, and I have no regrets. Each stage of my life prepared me for the next level of understanding. Had I not gone through the back and forth with my exes, I never would have been inspired to share my experience, or get to the bottom of my foundational issues. The breakup motivated me to open my life to a whole new way of living and surviving. More importantly, it ignited a burning desire to encourage people who are yearning for growth and independence all around the world.

Developing Stages in Life

There are many stages to life, and in each stage, changes are bound to occur. You must embrace these changes if you want to smoothly transition through each stage of your life. Each stage of life, as well as your healing, is a way to help you grow. You can not expect to jump from being wounded to a full recovery, at the drop of a dime because that's just unrealistic. It's also unrealistic to think that you can complete your healing by replacing your addiction with a rebound to avoid any pain. You only will carry the baggage of pain from one situation the next. I would recommend that you sort through your situation and get rid of your baggage of pain first. Pain is good when you are sacrificing for the betterment of your life. No pain, no gain! A masterpiece of greatness takes time to shape and mold. Every stage of life is just as important to your development as the stage of healing is to your recovery. This includes the hard times as well, because struggles build character. You should not want to skip any critical stages in life, because you will only cheat yourself of positive growth. You will know it is a critical stage when it takes a healthy dosage of determination, dedication, and perseverance to get through it. By avoiding your challenges, you choose the easy way out and overlook your lessons, which results in stunting your growth.

Stages of Life—Truly Letting Go

Imagine life as a child. What if you never developed the understanding of human or social interaction in society? As an adult, you probably would have a phobia of meeting other people outside of your comfort zone and you would have difficulty communicating, both physically and verbally. What about a growing adolescent? How would life be for you if you skipped through the challenges of transitioning into adulthood? You probably would have difficulty separating childlike behavior and adult responsibilities. What about grade school? Hypothetically speaking, what if you skipped seven grades, and went from the fifth grade to the twelfth grade? You would have severe difficulty functioning at this level because you skipped pivotal developmental stages. There is absolutely no way you would be able to function productively in life without first going through the natural stages of life. This same principle applies to your personal and professional development. Each stage prepares you for independence and teaches you how to understand who you truly are, and what you need to make you happy without dependency. Your growth in life is determined by the stages you have passed successfully; your healing is the same way. Even when it feels as though the easier way is to conform to familiarity, and assume a lackadaisical approach, just remember that you have to successfully get through your stages of life if you want growth. When this happens, you will make fewer excuses and mistakes for yourself, and your life becomes more productive. You will have minimum regrets, if any at all.

WOUNDED *by* BETRAYAL

Carry Your Cross

I saw a cartoon clip some time ago that provided a message without words. There were about 10 characters traveling by foot, each carrying a large cross of equal size, into the mountains. You could tell by the sweat and expressions of all the characters that they were struggling to carry their crosses to a destination unknown. The next pictures depicted one of the characters falling to his knees tired, as if to show that he could not bear his cross because it was too heavy. Hands clasped together, and looking to the sky, he began praying to a higher power to lighten his load. The next pictures showed the character cutting a large piece of his cross down before continuing on with his walk. The same character fell to his knees a second time praying for more relief, while the others continued walking. Again, he cut another large piece of his cross, making it even shorter and lighter. He then continued walking. Soon, all of the characters had reached a point in their journey where they could no longer walk because of a huge gap between two mountains. They had nowhere to turn, but clearly their journey was not over yet. Scratching their heads, one character decided to utilize his cross to bridge him to the other side, and the others followed in suit. The cartoon ended when all of the characters utilized their long, heavy, and durable crosses to bridge the gap to the other side of the mountain and complete their journey. However, the one character that had chosen not to bear his cross, by cutting pieces off, did not have enough cross to bridge him over to the other side. He was left alone, unable to move forward in his journey because of his choice to avoid the struggles in his journey. Be careful of what you wish or ask to receive, and mindful of the energy which is requesting what you desire.

Even when you are not sure of your destination, exercise faith to endure your struggles in order to allow your experiences to successfully bridge you over to the next stage of life. Value each lesson learned in your stages of life and embrace your experiences, because they will help prepare you for your next challenge in life. As explained in earlier chapters, it is normal to experience grief, anger, despair, emptiness, aloneness, temptation, and frustration in order to find peace, happiness, and freedom. It is simply the growing stages, molding you into the person you will need to be to protect your own interests once healed.

EACH STAGE IS A BUILDING LESSON TO YOUR GROWTH:

- Without experience, there wouldn't be growth.
- Without the grief, you wouldn't have noticed your unhappiness.
- Without anger, you wouldn't have become fed up.
- Without despair, you wouldn't have been provoked to search for hope.
- Without emptiness, you wouldn't be able to refill and rebuild yourself with positive assurance.
- Without aloneness, you wouldn't have found the time to learn yourself, or realize your true value.

- Without temptation, you wouldn't have a challenge.
- Without frustration, you wouldn't have accountability.
- Without peace, you wouldn't have found contentment within yourself.
- Without those experiences, you wouldn't have found happiness and freedom.

Embrace your story and every experience, but remember to make choices that will enhance your life.

Moving on to Chapter 8

CHAPTER 8

Dating Again

WELCOME TO DATING 101!

*E*ventually, you will start dating again, and this stage of your life should be welcomed. Dating can be a lot of fun, especially when there is no pressure involved. The purpose of dating is to get a good feel for what type of person you are compatible with. What better way to find out what you like, in a companion, than to open your horizons to the dating scene? Get out there and socialize to get a vibe for your needs, from a healed perspective of life, but understand there are roles to be played, and rules to be made, and followed, while dating. It is very important that you understand your role and boundaries to dating, in order to avoid getting caught up with the wrong individual. If the person has the potential opportunity to interact with you on a level that influences your affection, then it is crucial you scan the possible candidate for compatibility, before he influences you. You should remain attentive and alert in order to discern:

- If he assists in propelling or declining your growth. Can you see yourself growing around this person?
- If he qualifies to be in your company and personal space. What are his motives? Are they positive or negative, productive or destructive; is he playing games or is he serious?
- If he ventures for the same, or similar, outcome as you. Is he on the same page, in the same book, or near the same genre of what you want?
- If he truly is **_available_** for screening of possible compatibility. Is the person single?

While dating, you have to realize what is conducive and what will be detrimental to you. Hold your date to the same standard that you would hold yourself to, if not higher. If you sense bitterness and resentment in your date, allow him time to rid himself of the baggage before blindly walking into a situation with him. Think about it, were you ready to date after your devastating breakup, when you carried baggage and resentment? Open your eyes, and watch out for those telltale signs. You do not want to be anyone's rebound or easy prey. It would not be fair to you to fall into assuming the rebound role after you have just come out of your healing. I realize that you may find your life's partner in your dating encounters, but please keep in mind that the sole purpose of dating does not necessarily mean that you are on the hunt for your lifetime partner, as much as it is to build comfort and perspective when relating to a potential romantic interest on a platonic level. Therefore, again, be mindful of what company you choose to allow into your personal space, because your dating encounters very well may **not** be the lucky pick of the draw. Remember to do your homework before you allow someone to come in and sweep you off your feet. Some things simply have no business in your mix. Just go in with the thought process of, "I hope I have fun," instead of, "I hope this is the one." Expect nothing less and nothing more. When you view dating in this manner, you will be more relaxed and able to have fun without appearing *thirsty* (slang term for desperate). This way, if the date isn't going the way you would have wanted, you will have the courage to speak up without thinking that you messed this one up. Better yet, you will not feel discouraged as if you are growing further away from securing a partner because you voiced how you truly felt. You must remember that you owe it to yourself to express what you truly feel. Trust me, it will come out sooner than later, and it is better now than later, to avoid getting tangled in a situation that may be difficult to escape. You can speak up and still get your point across in a tactful, direct, but classy way.

Now, for the Rules!

I can not make it anymore simpler than this:

Rule #1: Don't be desperate.

Desperation is an unattractive trait. Desperation is a sure sign that you are not ready to represent yourself in a fashion that has your best interests at heart. Desperation equals easy prey, and you become an easy target to the hunters out there, those who are seeking their next kill.

Rule #2: Set your rules and stick to them.

Set realistic rules by which to abide. Rules and boundaries protect your interests so you don't get caught up too soon before knowing what you are getting yourself into. Without rules and boundaries, you could find yourself making unwise and emotionally rash decisions based on excitement. Whatever rule you set at the beginning should apply across the board, regardless of the effect the person happens to have on you. I know you may feel tempted to bend for a person for whom you feel instant chemistry, who seems to be perfect, have sexy swagger, or is just flat-out on point, but you can not allow all that charm to cloud your judgment. The same way you treat a person you are not feeling is the same way you should treat a person you are feeling. Nobody gets special privileges. Every candidate should be dealt with on the same level, until they earn the right to move up to the next level of comfort with you. Make them respect your rules, but more importantly, you need to respect them, too. Remember accountability. Exercise maturity by holding yourself accountable to your own guidelines.

Rule #3: Respect yourself and your date.

Respect always will take you a long way. Maintain your dignity through the respect you exude and give to others. Show your date how you expect to be treated by the way you treat and interact with others, including yourself. This will allow your date to get an idea of what he/she is dealing with and what caliber of class you are on, without you ever having to say a word. Respect is earned, so don't mandate or expect any more respect than you are willing to give.

Rule #4: Build friendships first.

Focusing on friendship promotes an honest and genuine relationship, which is needed to build a solid foundation for any connection. By doing so, you show potential mates that you are interested in getting to know them for who they are, and not for what they have to offer; which is what friendships are supposed to be based. Don't force anything for the purpose of landing romance before getting to really know the person. The connection should be natural. When you go in with the mindset of building a romantic relationship before friendship, you increase the chances of hindering the natural stages of possible progression. Focusing on a relationship first clouds your judgment, making it difficult to recognize any telltale signs, and you blindly set yourself up for possible failure by overlooking the otherwise intolerable flaws. Give yourself the time to find out if you can build a friendship without romance before you jump into anything more. After all, friendships normally last longer than lovers.

Rule #5: *Be honest about your intentions.*

Be open about what you want from your date. Let him know what role he is playing in your life, so as to avoid any misunderstandings. It's okay to date just for the conversation. Every date doesn't have to progress to romance, so don't feel guilty if your date is ready to advance to the next level and you are not. Move at a speed that is most comfortable for you and don't feel bad about doing so. Remember, it's okay to express that you are uncomfortable or unsure about something.

Rule #6: *Don't expose too much, too soon.*

Mystery sparks curiosity. Try to stay mysterious by protecting your privacy. In time, reveal what you deem appropriate. It's for your own protection. Until you can really trust the person and are confident that you are ready to progress into something serious, I would suggest you guard yourself.

Rule #7: *Have Fun!*

Don't put so much emphasis and pressure on your dates for something serious, and please don't hold your feelings on your shoulders by expecting every date to be "the one." You will disappoint yourself more times than not, and give up sooner than you should on dating. Just expect to have genuine fun; that's it! You should want your company to enhance your adventures in life!

Dating Again

BLIND DATE

This was one of my favorite stages in my journey because it was fun to date from a very different perspective. I mainly was interested in having fun without compromising myself in the process. I felt more like a woman, instead of a girl trying to find her way in the romance world. It was amazing to learn how men viewed me as a woman. I went in prepared, knowing that I was mature enough to understand the rules behind dating because I had gone through the necessary stages of maturity. I knew what to expect and what not to tolerate. Respect was the name of the game! I went in respecting myself and the person I happened to be dating at the time.

I linked up with my first date through a family friend. I explained to my friend that I simply was ready to get back on the dating scene, and asked if she knew of anyone for a blind date. It was my trial run. I had never been on a blind date before, but I figured asking for one would help me keep things in perspective, just in case I found that I was not ready for it. I specifically asked her for this favor because she understood what type of person I was, and I knew she would not purposely jeopardize my recovery. I told her that I simply wanted communication, nothing too serious or complicated, just someone to share quality time with, in good nature. She went to work for me and found me a single, young, and aspiring neurologist. In the past, that type of esteemed profession would have intimidated me, or made me nervous, because I would have had too much pressure trying to be perfect to win my date over. In this case, I was cool because I was not looking to land a serious relationship and I certainly was not thirsty for one. Had he been a volunteer worker at the local animal shelter, it would not have mattered, because I was only in it for the experience and conversation, not for any incentives that his profession potentially could do for me. Either way, both dates would have seen the same me. It was about making genuine friends and having fun! At first, the guy agreed to go out with me, but he did not contact me until a month later. He emailed me to introduce himself and to set up a time to meet. I happened to be out of town at the time he contacted me, but we agreed to go out once I returned. Two weeks later, I returned back to town and called him to set up a good time for the date. Our conversation lasted about 25 minutes, but I made certain not to ask too many questions because I really wanted it to be a blind date, and I did not want to prejudge him. We decided to meet at a local restaurant for lunch, nothing too extravagant or tacky.

This particular afternoon, the weather was freezing cold as showers of rain fell from the sky. I bundled up in a warm coat, scarf, gloves, and earmuffs. Under my coat was a thick sweater and some casual jeans, with a pair of knee-high boots covering the lower portion of my jeans. I finished my look with some neutral-colored eye shadow and a clear gloss on my lips. My hair was pulled back in loose curls that fell to my mid back. I was casual looking. He arrived a little early and was waiting on me in the parking lot. He spotted me as soon as I turned into the driveway, and our eyes connected. After I parked, he met me at my vehicle before I could get out, with an umbrella. I thought that was very sweet. He was wearing a Burberry newsboy cap, and a black scarf to keep warm. Underneath the scarf, he rocked a sweater vest, white shirt, black tie, slacks, and some black casual boots. He looked nice, like a smart, well-put-together pretty boy. After he opened my door, I stepped out of the car, stood next to him, and could not help but notice that my heels placed me a tad bit taller than him, which is normally a no-go for me. I typically want to feel protected in a relationship, and I normally have difficulty securing that comfort if I have to look down or face-to-face at my date, standing at 5'2". In this case, his height did not matter much to me because my intentions were not to land a husband. The moment we met, his facial expression showed that he was flattered but intimidated all in the same look. I guessed he expected me to be shorter. I was calm, comfortable, and had no major expectations or pressure to impress him.

He, on the other hand, appeared to be under a lot of pressure. He seemed tense in all his reactions, for reasons that were unclear to me. I continued to maintain a relaxed persona, so as to show him that I had no pre-existing expectations of the date, in the hopes that he would relax. He still could not seem to relax. It was as if he was walking on pins and needles, trying to figure out how to impress me. His conversation ranged from his current aspirations, to his undying respect for women, to how he enjoyed my company and felt instant chemistry, to his ex-girlfriend, all on the first date. He used the chemistry he claimed to feel for me as his reason for opening up to me so soon. He was all over the place. Our conversation, for the most part, went fairly well until he mentioned his recent one-month-old breakup. He even asked me about my last relationship, but I felt it was way too soon to have that conversation. That was a conversation I had no desire to expose to a complete stranger, so I informed him that I wished to reserve that topic for a different timeframe. I have learned that when you expose the intimate details of your previous relationship, you surrender both positive and negative leverage to the potential new partner. I think it's best to start with a new slate, without revealing the pieces to your puzzle too soon. However, my reservations about the topic did not stop my date from continuing on about his ex, and so he picked up where he left off. It spoke volumes to me that he was unable to separate the appropriateness of his conversation, especially considering my remark as to why I had decided not to speak about my last breakup. It was clear that he needed to vent, so I listened and let him vent, as I feasted over my tasty, sizzling-hot grilled chicken, mashed potatoes, and steamed broccoli!

At the conclusion of the date, I began deciphering his place in my circle of entertainment. I knew he was off-limits and unavailable to seriously pursue, but I was beginning to wonder if he was worth another date, for many reasons. One reason was that I knew he had some obvious healing to do emotionally, and I was not quite sure if he was available, or open, to a "friends-only" relationship with a woman. I discerned that he eagerly was searching for a replacement because his whole aura seemed desperate. I felt as though he was either under pressure to really land a connection, or he had something to hide. I thought about why he over polluted our first

Dating Again

date by talking about his recent ex and their bad experiences. Perhaps he was still in a healing process. He had nothing good to say about her, but everything good to say about himself. I thought that was tacky. All of those signs were turnoffs for me. I probably would have looked right past all of those telltale signs, had my focus been on feeding my desire of needing a man, or if I was still wounded by betrayal. When your focus becomes compromised, and someone throws you some bait, usually you take it without considering the dangers. In this case, I did not let his supposed feeling of chemistry trick me into igniting some type of favor for him. I held true to my focus and considered all aspects of the date.

Though I strongly felt that we were not a match, he asked to go out again later in the week. I agreed, figuring I would give it another chance. Maybe he was not good at being himself on first dates and perhaps we could be friends. This time we met up for dinner. He was a little more relaxed and exposed a few more things about himself that were red flags for me. Midway through dinner, I knew for certain that I could not entertain any romantic possibilities. At this point, I was trying to figure out his role in my life. I wondered if he remained in my life in the capacity of a friend, whether he would enhance or decline my growth. Either way, I decided to pay for our meal this time, but I had to make my intentions clear to him after he insisted on paying. I expressed to him that I did not consider us to be dating anymore, and therefore it probably would not be fair to him to wine and dine me under that assumption. It was my pleasure to pay; after all, he paid last time. He said he respected my honesty and appreciated my efforts in trying to create balance to what could possibly blossom into a friendship. Later, I found out this guy was not a citizen of the United States and needed to earn citizenship very soon, otherwise he would have to face deportation and would lose his chance at completing his education in the States. That information helped me to realize his motives and why he appeared bitter and desperate. He was so close to getting what he needed, but his ex-girlfriend and soon to-be wife left him, pushing him further from his personal goals. I then understood his motivation at trying so hard to impress me. In the end, I decided I did not want this particular person in my circle of entertainment because I was not willing to offer him what he wanted. It seemed as if I was in a constant battle of defending my personal space with him, even though he knew I only intended to be friends. Finally, I aborted all communication altogether when he proposed paying me $5,000 to marry him, in order for him to remain in the States. In the past, I would have looked right past the flaws in order to secure a serious mate and fall in love again. I would have thought him to be the perfect connection, too, since he was just as eager to get into something serious real soon. By the time I would have uncovered the real motivation, it would have been too late.

Though in this particular case, my date was the needy, desperate one, I've walked that road where I assumed the desperate role. I could tell the guys sensed my neediness. I came across one particular guy who wanted someone who had it together and could stand solid as an individual. I could tell he was completely turned off by my neediness. The more I tried, the more he ignored or avoided me. Granted, I was not ready yet, but honestly, if a person isn't interested, don't go out of your way to convince them otherwise. Please remember, if a person shows no sign of interest, especially after you express your interest, chances are they do not have that spark in their eye for you. It does not mean you are not good enough, it just means it is not for you.

Just be Yourself

Stay consistent in your behavior, but more importantly, don't do anything you don't plan to continue throughout the life of the friendship. Often, people get caught up with trying to impress their dates, but find themselves in a tight bind when these things become expected and they can not deliver. If you don't like certain things, let it be known. If you like certain luxuries, by all means, let that be known, too. Don't act like you are used to certain luxuries and *expect* your date to shower you with gifts you can not even afford to buy for yourself; that wouldn't be fair. Don't pretend you like certain things when you really don't, just to impress your date. Give yourself a chance to be accepted for who you really are and not what you think your date wants, or expects. It should be easier to deliver a genuine personality than a fake one. I stressed the importance of properly working through your stages because you truly can be yourself once you find out who you are. That's why it's so important to find yourself before you attempt to accomplish anything else. Being real from the start gives each of you a chance to see if you can be comfortable with each other's beliefs, interest, appearance, lifestyle, and personality.

Have Fun

Don't be uptight; it's one of the rules. You have taken yourself out before; dating should be a piece of cake. View dating as a way to enjoy those same outings, but now with company. Try stepping outside of your comfort zone by dating outside of your usual type. I remember dining with a guy who told me that his last date was looking for a six-foot, light-skinned dude with dreadlocks. He was the exact opposite of that description, standing about 5'4", with a chocolate complexion, and a low-fade haircut. He simply wished her well because her hope to find someone who matched her ex was not a competition he wanted to enter. This guy happened to be a really great catch, but the girl did not see it because she was too busy looking for a tall, light-skinned guy with dreadlocks. Expect to meet different people, of different cultures, and of different sizes. I encourage you to go on dates with people to whom you are not physically attracted. This will train you to see the heart of a person. You have to train yourself to see the heart of the matter so that you do not fall for physical attraction only. Outer beauty fades away, but the heart maintains its beauty. As such, you need to learn how to mingle on different levels with good, genuine people.

Dating Again

Take some time out to laugh, play, and make game playing a priority in your dating experiences. Challenge each other in video, board, and card games. Try a little outdoor activity like sports, and include other people in your fun. How about touch football or track racing? These are all great ways to learn more about your date. It doesn't always have to be dinner and a movie to be considered dating. Honestly, how much are you really getting to know about the person if you are watching a movie that you must sit quietly through? Creative dating is healthy for the development of your bond. I have been able to discover personality traits in a simple game of checkers with some of the guys I initially met on a date. During the game, some became very competitive, and one was very aggressive when he lost, which was something I needed to see. He repeatedly called himself "a stupid loser", which I thought was a bit harsh, but really became concerned when he began cursing himself aloud, and even punched himself when he lost a third straight game. I uncovered a temper that a normal dinner/movie date otherwise would have kept covered up. After a few competitive board games, I had discovered that this particular guy had anger management issues. I decided to number one, not ever play and beat him at another game of checkers again, especially alone, and number two, to get the heck out of dodge, fast! Aside from that one aggressive experience, strategy games typically challenge the brain and reveal creative pictures as to how well a person can think outside the box. For this reason, I was okay with introducing my new male acquaintances to a good game of checkers on an initial date. I was able to pick out their way of thinking by the choices they made, and what they gave up when options became limited on the game board. I always have a good time playing board games with new friends, and it is a great way to break the ice.

You even can make up a game. Ask each other questions, lots of questions! It can be a combination of serious questions mixed with playful, easy questions, so it does not feel too intense. The name of the game is "Get to know your Date." Of course, the more you hang out, the more you will learn, but it doesn't hurt to ask questions. See below a few of my questions!

- What's your favorite food?
- Do have a close relationship with your family?
- Would you ever skydive on a first date, if it was requested?
- What does the title "friends" really mean to you? Explain the dynamics.
- What's your favorite color?
- What are you looking for in a potential partner?
- Would you ever challenge me in an ice cream eating contest, if I dared you to?

Of course, you can choose a different selection of questions, but just remember your motive is to have fun while you get to know your new friend. Naturally, you will have to get a feel for your date's personality in order to ask appropriate questions for the occasion.

Dating Again

JUDGE

A guy I decided not to pursue criticized me on this subject. That experience actually encouraged me to include this section in the dating chapter. After asking a few questions about his background, he failed the first interview by lying about having five kids, by five different women. He lied because he did not want me to judge him. He thought it was not fair, and I thought it was unfair to attempt to build a connection on false pretenses and lies. I wanted the information in order to get to know him. Originally, he only admitted to having one kid, and tried to use his words to deceive me about the other four kids. Noticing his choice of wording, I reworded my question, so as to not leave him any room to attempt deceit with a little play on words game. He reluctantly answered he had a second child, but finally admitted to five children. He claimed his kids were private, and no one needed to know how many he really had. I figured him out quickly by judging his actions, and concluded that he did not have a place in my life. I knew what I wanted, and I knew what type of people I wanted to surround myself with. I had a zero tolerance for straight-up liars. Fortunately for me, I quickly discerned that this guy had many dark secrets that burdened his ability to live a happy, normal life. It appeared as though he was trying to use his strife as a way to gain sympathy and easy affection from me. I also had a zero tolerance for guys whose agenda was to get me in bed, lie to impress, or disregarded what I stood for in relation to my morals. I'm here to tell you that you should judge whether or not a person belongs in your sphere of influence or life. If you are going to be investing a considerable amount of interest and time with the person, then you should be the judge to determine if he is worth your time. Don't get me wrong, I'm not saying you should judge his fate to heaven or hell, but judge him to the degree of determining whether or not he is compatible to you or the lifestyle you are working towards. In other words, don't give anyone the opportunity to pull you down with their issues. Pick and choose out of logic, discernment, and love for yourself, not out of desperation, guilt, or because you were convinced. By all means, never go against your better judgment.

While we're on the subject of judging, don't allow your eyes to guide your judgment, either. Instead, utilize your sense of intuition and study the person. You are way too valuable to offer yourself to the wolves in the name of satisfaction. You have to value yourself enough to take your time and not throw it all in, showing everything you have to offer, and making yourself vulnerable to disappointment. By this time, you should be humble enough to walk away if the person doesn't meet your standards or isn't compatible to you. You **do not** have to settle. Dating is a luxury, not a necessity. Though your goal may be to find another form of happiness in companionship, it is very important that you not join your accomplishments to a potential adversary. Don't let the ignorance of someone else bring you down. Don't try changing someone who doesn't want to be changed just to meet your desires, either. You still have more growing to do, so do not slow down to live for someone else who doesn't have your best interest at heart.

Dating Again

TELLTALE SIGNS

Look out for the telltale signs. Wandering eyes tell you that they lack discipline, especially if it's right in front of you. I find it quite disrespectful to be on an outing where my date constantly checks out every woman who walks in the building. It's one thing to look, but it's quite another to goggle with no hint of restraint. This may not be an issue for some, but I have learned that people, who can not control their eyes, typically can not control their cravings. Remember, when you have a healthy focus and appetite, the outer attributes don't catch your attention as strongly as the heart does. How much they are willing to invest in you will determine what you mean to them. I am referring to time, initiative, and intent, since this is the beginning stage of your connection. Anyone can invest money, jewels, and lavish vacations, when they have them. When a person invests his time and makes strong and genuine efforts in you, you will know that he is investing his heart with good intent. Money and gifts have nothing to do with the endurance of one's heart. I would encourage you not to confuse gifts, money, and affection for real love, if you can not get the person's respect, time, and initiative. Respect, time, and genuine efforts normally reveal the heart of the matter.

Whatever the person is willing to do with you now, before he knows you, he probably would be willing to do with anyone. What makes you more special than anyone else? Pay attention to how much he is willing to give up so soon? Does he value himself? You do not want someone who does not value himself, because you will not be compatible, and he probably will have a hard time respecting your progress. Essentially, he will work as the weaker link to your progression. Another telltale sign to pay close attention to is flirtation. Is it pure and respectful, or lustful and sleazy? Does the person see your heart or your outer attributes? You want someone who can see and appreciate your inner beauty. There, he will find your value and protect it through this appreciation. Be careful not to invest in a superficial person. If all it takes is the aesthetic attributes to win the person over, imagine what the next-best-looking thing will do once you change or become old? Someone always will be prettier, smarter, or more interesting, but no one will ever have the same heart as you. Your heart is your treasure and it is what makes you so unique. That gives you all the more reason to guard your heart from foolishness. Keep your heart pure, because it is what will attract you to like kinds, and allow you to decipher who does not belong in your life.

Sex

My brother Gabriel and I had a conversation regarding the open approach many people take when it comes to sex and sharing sexual partners. We shared similar views on the topic, and I thought it would be great to share them with you. We both agreed that, even though sex is supposed to be the gift you give to your partner to express the love you already should feel, many people have sex thinking it will make them fall in love. Below was my brother's opinion on the whole matter. I hope this adds as much value to your view on sex as much as it did to mine.

> *"I think as men, no, as human beings, we should prove that we are more than just mammals by practicing restraint and balance. If you are willing to sacrifice what is supposed to be the most important thing in your life for a moment of pleasure, then you have a problem. Sex can be an addiction that is as destructive as alcoholism or drug addictions. Just like any other addiction, the first step to defeating it is recognizing it as unnatural. Yes, we all have cravings, but they have to be controlled, especially if it's going to hurt those you love and live for."*

For the sake of healing, I recommend abstinence during your journey, especially during the early stages. Sexual promiscuity has a very strong and addictive nature. It would be rather unwise to involve yourself sexually with someone just because you like them or are lonely. Sex is supposed to be the most intimate gift you can share with someone worthy of touching your soul. As a person striving for unity, stability, honesty, and happiness, once you have truly found happiness, celibacy will not be as hard as many may believe it to be. Practicing restraint and celibacy can help prepare you for the long haul commitment in marriage. I do believe that once a person is stripped from of all of their greed, distractions, and selfishness, then they will realize what is most important to life, and then they will truly start to live life in its entirety. I believe commitment is not just a word or act; rather, it is the mere respect for **faith**. Learn to commit to healthy living and healthy living will commit to you.

Not Ready to Date yet?

I understand there may be some out there who may want companionship, but are not ready to date yet. Not to worry, there are other alternatives to dating. Perhaps you want to have fun and enjoy outdoor activities with company, but not quite ready to get back into the dating scene yet. Try getting a pet. Nurturing and supporting an animal gives you responsibility and ownership. The responsibility of a pet will provide you the feeling of being needed and loved because a pet needs its owner to survive. Therefore, go out and buy yourself a dog, cat, fish, or whatever you feel will provide you the company you desire. As you watch your pet grow from the nourishment you provide, you should feel a sense of dual accomplishment. The love and care you gave to your pet is like a reflection of the love you give yourself to nurture your healing. Your pet will depend on you for survival, and so should you to yourself. You need to be able to count on yourself to get you through tough stages in your life.

Conclusion

Dating can be fun, but like anything else, it also can get old and boring to you. If you date with the intentions suggested in this chapter, dating will remain fun and become an extension of your happiness, the happiness you already should have. Stay in control of yourself while dating, and don't make ill-advised and premature decisions out of excitement. Keep things in perspective, and pay attention to the way your company makes you feel once you have separated yourself from the engagement. If you separate feeling drained, unmotivated, and bad overall, then something is wrong. You should not feel negative energy after what should be a positive social event. More than likely, this person will not enhance your journey, and you should rethink whether or not this person should be in your arena of social interaction. However, if the person makes you feel energized, uplifted, and good overall, then that is your sign that you have found good company for yourself. Watch out for emotional spurts of energy, as they sometimes have been known to cause your limbic system to release an exceptionally large amount of endorphins to catch you off guard, and make you think you are either in love or intoxicated. This state can cause you to say or do things that are inappropriate or premature at the time. A good rule of thumb is to manage your decisions wisely. Even if you are not ready to step out and explore your horizons, position yourself to be ready. Check yourself at the beginning, and stick to your demands by drafting some rules of your own to dating. You know what you need to make you happy. Don't depend on anyone or anything else but yourself to fulfill your life. If you compromise your principles and well-being for emotional satisfaction, you are settling.

Your desire for companionship should not override your good

judgment. If you cannot make logical decisions based on what is best for you, then you are not ready for dating. However, if you can make logical decisions based on what you know is best for you, then go out and have fun!

CHAPTER 9

Life Goes On

ROUTINE MAINTENANCE FOR GUARANTEED SATISFACTION

One of the best things about life is that you can change it whenever you want, especially if you are unsatisfied. What's even better is that you don't need a companion, or validation of any sort to make that happen for you. Satisfaction is a personal decision and achievement, and the choices you make determine the outcome of your satisfaction. When you live to make choices that are satisfying to your spirit, which lives within, you will also find that happiness is an internal, personal decision. Even after you have completed your healing, and you are living a life that is satisfying your current needs, you will have to perform routine maintenance to remain satisfied. It's just like owning a new car; you can not keep driving it without performing the routine maintenance, such as an oil change, spark plug checks, tire rotation, or internal/external cleaning. If you choose to continue driving your car without servicing, it eventually will break down, get old quickly, and become useless after a while, all because of the lack of simple, routine maintenance.

If you want things to properly serve you, you must properly service them. This is also the case for your own life and your relationships. I'm referring to all of your relationships (e.g. friends, colleagues, partners, family or spouse), if they play a significant role in your life. Keep all of your relationships healthy, by simply refreshing your connections with positive reinforcement along the way. Whenever I get discouraged or feel that my journey in life is in need of a tune-up, I remind myself of the big picture, and then revisit the plans that I originally mapped out to reach my goals. By revisiting my plans, I get the invigoration and renewed drive that I need to continue pursuing my goals ceaselessly. I also relive some of my old adventures. I'll tell ya, jumping out of an airplane has a distinct way of instantaneously sparking revival in my life! Those are just a couple of things I found that works for me because I am the adventurous type and I know what moves me. Find out what motivates you and utilize it to maintain your drive for the future.

As you move on in life, you have to remember to keep everything about your life fresh. Only you can determine what is best for you because you should know you best. The reason I emphasized the importance of getting to know yourself during the healing process was to prepare you for life after healing. As explained in Chapter 4, when you understand yourself, you get to know what it takes to make and keep you happy, but more importantly, why it keeps you happy. This awareness also provides the final puzzle piece to what you need to maintain good, spiritual health after recovery, in order to nurture your relationships, and for sustained satisfaction in your life. I make it a duty to balance my life with quiet meditation, personal time, social time, family time, and spiritual time. I also pay attention to my actions and the driving force that provokes my actions. I want to make sure I'm aware of what I'm exposing myself to and which of my desires needs to be nourished or starved, and you should too. It is critical to your life to maintain a strong, healthy spirit and check for unhealthy desires in your routine maintenance checkups. Catering to your fleshly desires can weaken your spirit, cripple your growth, and push you back into an addictive lifestyle. Instead, make it your obligation to expose your spirit to things that will feed and strengthen its will, even after healing, by:

- Denying the flesh of unhealthy desires.
- Guarding what you feed and expose your mind and body to (e.g. music, people, and entertainment).
- Confessing your faults and acknowledging your weaknesses.
- Maintaining high integrity by doing the right thing even when no one is looking.
- Positive exposure through support systems, self-help literature, or vision-oriented people.

- Fasting and prayer, meditation, and self-reflection.
- Loving and forgiving.

Once you are aware of what it takes to maintain a healthy spirit, you are able to steer your dreams in the direction most suitable for guaranteed satisfaction. When you strengthen and refresh your spirit with routine maintenance, you will experience fulfillment. Your life can be filled with joy and freedom simply by doing what it takes to maintain balance and peace. It is imperative that we learn to deny our fleshly desires, to position ourselves to live for the spirit, where we will find ultimate satisfaction.

Flesh vs. Spirit

Those who live according to the flesh have their minds set on what the flesh desires, but those who live in accordance with the spirit have their minds set on what the spirit desires. We have no obligation to be dominated by human nature. We must not live to satisfy our fleshly desires. If you live according to your human nature, you are going to die, but if, by the spirit, you put to death your sinful actions, you will live.

(Romans 8: 9, 12-13)

As you move on in your new life, make decisions based on how it will affect your spirit instead of your flesh. Living for the flesh enslaves you to the unhealthy desires rendered by human nature. I believe unhealthy desires and addictions are all extensions and motivations of the flesh. When you live according to your spirit, you are able to overcome your temptation and exercise discipline, which results to ultimate freedom. When you understand what is morally right to your beliefs and compatible to your new journey, you can determine if your decisions are based from the flesh or the spirit.

Structure is necessary for the well-being of our spirit. Succumbing to society's way of living, if it does not agree with you, will change your view of healthy living. So, continue to hold true to your beliefs and views once you have healed. Don't let disappointments change you for the worst, and never lose yourself for temporary pleasures. Think your decisions through and make wise choices based on your well-being, and not of the flesh. This will take much sacrifice, but sacrifice is good when it is done with purpose and against sinful nature. The lessons will teach you how to put many things in perspective.

FREEDOM IN FORGIVENESS

You will know that you have found freedom when you are ready to forgive anything that has caused you to feel either betrayed or abandoned. This includes yourself, if you were the sole source to your downfall. Propel your healing by forgiving, and allow your experiences to help you grow deeper in wisdom. When you are able to forgive, you allow yourself to become resistant to past disappointments because you have learned to let it go and it does not affect you any longer. Remove any obstacles in place that may be keeping you from forgiving, in order to experience the freedom that you deserve. Through forgiveness, you will be set free!

END TO MY EXES

Eventually, I moved on and got over my first, second, and third ex. It took me going to war with my flesh, and I had to fight through all of my desires, including the desire to contact my exes or jump into another unhealthy situation. Through constant denial, and very strong willpower, eventually, my flesh weakened and the force subsided. Abstinence provoked intense soul-searching, and I finally was able to see clearly, without the distraction of my fleshly desires. I had starved the flesh and finally was able to detach from the unhealthy desires that were plaguing my progress. I was left empty inside. I had let go of everything in order to find solitude and locate my inner strength. I let go of my old understanding of success, and the priority I had given relationships, and the possibility of marriage, over my wellbeing because they contributed to my decline. I knew I had to let go, and rearrange my priorities, because I was living for relationships and the possibilities attached to them, but at the expense of my emotional stability. By letting go, I gained everything; I gained my freedom. Life is a lot easier now that I no longer compromise my happiness. My conscience is clear, and I trust my decisions, because I know that my best interest is truly at heart. My happiness no longer is camouflaged in things that grant temporary satisfaction. When you reach the point where you love strengthening your spirit more than the desire to feed your flesh, you will know that you have made it. You will be able to move on successfully with your life, passing any test life shall present to you.

As expected, my first love married after our last conversation, and decided that, out of respect for his wife, it would be best if we ceased all communication. I respected his decision, and have not seen him since our breakup. Years later, I learned that he remains happily married with children, and we still do not speak, out of respect for his wife and family.

My second ex says that he casually dates from time to time, but ultimately remains single and comfortable in his position. Over the years, we were able to patch up our differences, tolerate each other's views, and build a platonic friendship. Today, we communicate sporadically, and he still claims that he is absolutely heterosexual.

My third ex and I attempted to make it work one last time after a nine-month split. This time, I knew only two things could happen: either we would run strong together (provided that he had changed) or we would end it once and for all. We decided to spend a week together, and met off the coast of Venezuela. After spending so much time apart, I was able see what I was dealing with in him. He never had any intention to secure a solid relationship, and I needed my closure. I hoped for the best, but planned for the worst, and knew that, whatever the outcome would be, it had to be permanent. After my arrival, I found that he was still addicted to promiscuity and habitual lying, and was not interested at all in forming anything serious with just one person. I was disappointed, greatly, to find that he had not changed, but more, I was relieved that I did not have to hope for *us* any longer. After that reunion, I got the closure that I needed. It was absolutely clear that we had no future together, so I wished him well, and we went our separate ways. I have not seen him since.

Maintaining Happiness

I believe that true love is enduring, patient, selfless, and unique. Pure love has the power to balance and satisfy every burning desire that one ever could have. I finally have found pure love in myself, and it sustains me daily. Today, I live, by choice, alone. Do I want companionship? Yes, of course, but I do not want to settle for someone who isn't mature enough to understand the dynamics of genuine love. We should be willing to wait as long as we have to, so as not to compromise our happiness. We also should be willing to wait for a partner who respects us and holds us in the highest regard. After all, if we never unite with that partner, at least we are left with a positive and fulfilling life. I would rather that then settle for someone incompatible to me.

My life isn't so bad that I must surrender to destruction in the name of temporary satisfaction. I have found happiness in my life, and it is not defined by the people surrounding it. I love that I, independently, live life comfortably with just being me. It took a lot of time and forgiveness to reach this level of freedom, but I am here to tell you that it is very much possible. I am a regular person who simply was determined to find security in my own happiness, and I believed in myself. That drive drove me away from addictive desires. We are in control of our happiness, and it is everlasting. The willpower you have built over time to reach this happiness is the same willpower that will sustain your happiness, but you have to love yourself enough to wait for your healing to evolve. In case you are wondering how long this process will take, or at what point you have waited long enough to reach ultimate happiness, know this: You must wait as long as it takes until you lose the desire to surrender yourself for temporary pleasures. Give yourself time to blossom and mature into your new life. Set your bar, build your circle, and live your life based on your desires to be a better you.

Soon, this book will end, and you will turn the final page, but that does not mean it is the end to your healing. Life goes on no matter what decisions you make, but it is up to you if you move along with life or get left behind. Live your life with integrity, dignity, and purpose. Utilize what you have learned to make permanent change in your life. If you have to re-read this book again, then do so. If you must repeat chapters of this book before moving on to the next chapter of your life, then by all means, do whatever you have to do to reach your ultimate destination, but don't stop moving forward. Life always will bring about many challenges, some desirable and others less desirable. It is how you handle those challenges that determine the direction of your journey.

Take a stand for yourself *now*, in order to prepare for your future, and never look back. Let go of the nonsense and continue to move towards freedom because you can do whatever you set your mind to. Only you know your true limits, and you are the only person who can stop you from reaching your goals. As mentioned before, the battle does not end with this book, because life goes on. It ends the way you choose to complete your chapter. What will your final chapter read at the end of your journey? Continue moving towards success and freedom because giving up on *you* can never, ever be an option!

Welcome to your new beginning!

Acknowledgements

I can only give God the credit for my accomplishments and many, many, many blessings. I thank God for allowing me to complete this project, which is merely an extension of my heart.

To my daddy, **Don,** who is always a phone call away, ready to rescue me in my time of need. Daddy, you always have supported me in whatever decision I have made, and I thank you for always standing by my side. I'm sure it was not easy watching me go through heartbreak and not being able to protect me from the pain. You were right when you said that I did not fall in love overnight, and I certainly was not falling out of love overnight, either. I have always found comfort in your words, and knowing that you supported my every move made me feel as though I was never alone in my journey, because you were always with me, waiting to see the outcome of my decisions! It is a beautiful feeling to know that I *still* make you proud! Truth be told, I live for it! I love you, Daddy! You are the leading man of my life!

Mommy, my earthly mother, sister in Christ and best friend, *Mary*, I love you with all of my heart! I don't know where to begin to thank you. You have been the backbone to my every move, and have supported me with unconditional love and prayers. I love you for remaining by my side, even when you did not agree with my decisions. Every time I felt lost, your support added direction to my journey. I feel as though I forever will be indebted to you because there is nothing I can give to repay you for all that you have given to me. Love is an amazing gift! I love you, my best friend, and thank you for just being **you!**

To my one and only big sister, ***LaQuanda***, thank you for always believing in me and pushing me to lift my standards, then live up to my own principles, and lastly, for always reminding me to, "Never settle!" I have always admired your strength, creativity, and poise! I love you! *Sisters forever!*

To my brothers, my childhood bodyguards, each of you plays a unique role in my life, even as an adult, and I am very grateful to have four amazing brothers who love and cherish me with all of their hearts. I thank you all for schooling me on men, love, and relationships. I especially thank you all for protecting me as I grew from a child into womanhood. Your constant illustrations of what a man should be, forever will contribute to my foundational requirements. ***Don Jr.***, thank you for the support and love you always have showered on me. ***Gabriel***, thank you for your strict, fatherly love, and the direction you *forced* on me. You were always the one to push me into becoming a respectable woman, even though I did not understand it then; I do now. I will always remember your reminder that you are on the sidelines cheering me on to be my best and make the right decisions! You are truly an amazing big brother and a perfect father! Your guidance has helped me to become a responsible, confident woman today. ***Adonis*** (AKA "Billy-Bop"), thank you for always standing by my side, fighting for my well-being, and always believing in me. You are a masterpiece waiting to be unveiled to the world. Keep it up; the world will soon see your

Acknowledgements

talents. I believe in you! **Chris**, "my adventure buddy", thank you for looking up to me, because it pushed me to want to be an even better big sister! Thanks for exploring, with me, all of the crazy and adventurous ideas I keep coming up with. Next time, I'll let you push me out of the airplane! ☺ I love you guys! Together, you all are the men of my life!

To my sisters-in-law Tiffany and Candy, thank you for believing in "Wounded by Betrayal," and proofreading my manuscripts. Your support never will be forgotten. I could not ask for better sisters-in-law! Thank you, thank you, and thank you!

Special acknowledgements go to all 15 of my nieces and nephews: JaTyra, Terrell (Tank) Jr., JaDaven, JaKera, Lil Chris, JaDaihya, Jasilyn, Terren, Adonis Jr., Aryah, Taylyn, Akyse, Teghan, Alysah, and Alyjah, who continue to make me proud by making wise decisions for their future success. That's the best gift you could ever give me, your Nanny! I love each and every one of you with all my heart, and I only want the best for you all! I'm watching you!

To my good friend, Chibuzo "Dika" Emenike, where do I even begin to thank you? Honestly, words can not express my gratitude for your genuine friendship. You have been there for me like a big brother, working behind the scenes, looking out for me no matter where I was located in the world. You were there to comfort me during my heartbreaks and even there to rejoice with me after my healing. Thank you so much for always being there for me,–no matter what! I especially thank you for the endless hours of proof reading and helping me to meet my strict deadlines. Even when my deadlines seemed unreasonable and your schedule did not permit, you always carved out time to accommodate me. I have always enjoyed giving you a complicated explanation, and watching you turn it into a simple, well thought out sentence. Your patience is impeccable and I appreciate you tremendously for keeping in touch and being such an amazing friend to me. Much love to you, Dika.

To all those who assisted me in my project, from the photographers to the designers: Quentin Guillory with Q.Guillory Photography, Deshawn Taylor, Tunde "Ben" Awosanya, Ganga Tippani, Nakeii Washington, and Albert Sampson, thank you so much.

Lastly, I thank those who played both positive and negative roles in my life. By the grace of God, I was able to find the good in every experience, which helped mold me into a better woman. Forgiveness and love is what remains in my heart!

Love Always,
La'Donna R. Edmond

About the Author

La'Donna R. Edmond

Was born and raised in Beaumont, Texas, but now resides in Houston, Texas. She holds an MBA in Finance & Accounting, and, for over 6 years, has worked internationally, in the Middle Eastern / Central Asian region of the world encompassing Dubai (U.A.E), Afghanistan, Uzbekistan and Iraq.

She is an avid traveler who has visited over 15 countries around the globe. Traveling is just one of her many passions as she is also a singer/recording artist, an author, and entrepreneur. Most recently, she has turned her attention towards recording her debut album and audio book for *Wounded by Betrayal*.

La'Donna, a strong advocate for healthy living, utilizes her experiences and talents, however she can, to inspire and motivate people to live life healthily and optimally.

We want to hear from you. Please send your comments about this book by visiting: www.LADONNArEDMOND.com

Follow La'Donna R. Edmond on
Facebook, Twitter, YouTube and LinkedIn.

Like us on Facebook:
www.facebook.com/pages/LaDonna-R-Edmond
or
www.facebook.com/pages/Wounded-by-Betrayal-Author-LaDonna-R-Edmond

For bulk ordering please visit and submit your order request through www.LADONNArEDMOND.com.